ALSO BY HAROLD BLOOM

Iago: The Strategies of Evil

Lear: The Great Image of Authority

Cleopatra: I Am Fire and Air

Falstaff: Give Me Life

The Daemon Knows

The Shadow of a Great Rock:
A Literary Appreciation
of The King James Bible

The Anatomy of Influence:
Literature as a Way of Life

Till I End My Song:
A Gathering of Last Poems

Fallen Angels

American Religious Poems:
An Anthology

Jesus and Yahweh: The Names Divine

Where Shall Wisdom Be Found?

The Best Poems
of the English Language:
From Chaucer Through Frost

Hamlet: Poem Unlimited

Genius: A Mosaic of One Hundred
Exemplary Creative Minds

Stories and Poems for Extremely
Intelligent Children of All Ages

How to Read and Why

Shakespeare: The Invention
of the Human

Omens of Millennium

The Western Canon

The American Religion

The Book of J

Ruin the Sacred Truths

Poetics of Influence

The Strong Light of the Canonical

Agon: Towards a Theory
of Revisionism

The Breaking of the Vessels

The Flight to Lucifer:
A Gnostic Fantasy

Wallace Stevens:
The Poems of Our Climate

Figures of Capable Imagination

Poetry and Repression

A Map of Misreading

Kabbalah and Criticism

The Anxiety of Influence

The Ringers in the Tower:
Studies in Romantic Tradition

Yeats

Commentary on David V. Erdman's
Edition of The Poetry
and Prose of William Blake

Blake's Apocalypse

The Visionary Company

Shelley's Mythmaking

SHAKESPEARE'S PERSONALITIES

MACBETH

A DAGGER
OF THE MIND

HAROLD BLOOM

SCRIBNER

New York   London   Toronto   Sydney   New Delhi

Scribner

An Imprint of Simon & Schuster, Inc.
1230 Avenue of the Americas
New York, NY 10020

First Scribner trade paperback edition April 2020

SCRIBNER and design are registered trademarks of The Gale Group, Inc.,
used under license by Simon & Schuster, Inc., the publisher of this work.

For information about special discounts for bulk purchases,
please contact Simon & Schuster Special Sales at 1-866-506-1949
or business@simonandschuster.com.

The Simon & Schuster Speakers Bureau can bring authors to your live event.
For more information or to book an event contact the Simon & Schuster Speakers
Bureau at 1-866-248-3049 or visit our website at www.simonspeakers.com.

Interior design by Erich Hobbing

Manufactured in the United States of America

1   3   5   7   9   10   8   6   4   2

Library of Congress Control Number: 2018276715

ISBN 978-1-5011-6425-5
ISBN 978-1-5011-6426-2 (pbk)
ISBN 978-1-5011-6427-9 (ebook)

For Glen Hartley

Contents

Acknowledgments   xi

Author's Note   xiii

1: And Nothing Is, but What Is Not   1

2: False Face Must Hide What the False Heart Doth Know   7

3: A Dagger of the Mind, a False Creation   21

4: In the Great Hand of God I Stand   33

5: Tear to Pieces That Great Bond / Which Keeps Me Pale   49

6: We Are Yet but Young in Deed   61

7: What, Will the Line Stretch Out to th' Crack of Doom   77

8: Yet Who Would Have Thought the Old Man to Have Had So Much Blood in Him?   95

9: My Way of Life / Is Fallen into the Sere, the Yellow Leaf   121

10: The Time Is Free   133

Acknowledgments

I am happy to acknowledge my research assistant Alice Kenney, my publisher and editor Nan Graham, and my editors Tamar McCollom and Sean Devlin. My assistant Natalie Rose Schwartz helped greatly with revising the proofs.

For the last thirty years I have worked with my literary agents Glen Hartley and Lynn Chu. I have a particular debt to Glen Hartley, who suggested to me this sequence of five brief books on Shakespeare's personalities. For that and for much else, I dedicate this book to him.

Author's Note

I have tended to follow the latest Arden edition. However, I have repunctuated according to my understanding of the text. In some places, I have restored what I believe to be Shakespeare's language, whenever I judge traditional emendations to be in error.

MACBETH

A DAGGER
OF THE MIND

CHAPTER 1

And Nothing Is,
but What Is Not

Nietzsche asserts, in *The Dawn of Day*, that "whoever thinks that Shakespeare's theatre has a moral effect, and that the sight of Macbeth irresistibly repels one from the evil of ambition, is in error. . . . He who is really possessed by raging ambition beholds this its image, with *joy*; and if the hero perishes by his passion this is precisely the sharpest spice in the hot draught of this joy."

Shakespeare's cognitive powers are invested more abundantly in Hamlet than in any other personality, be it Falstaff, Rosalind, Cleopatra, Prospero. His proleptic and prophetic imagination possesses Macbeth, to a degree unmatched by anyone else in the dramas. Macbeth cannot keep up with his own intimations of the night world. No sooner does he envision an action than he leaps into futurity and gazes back at his initial impulse. Macbeth is a weird, an involuntary soothsayer. The Weird Sisters inevitably await him, knowing that he is, in part, their kin.

Readers quite possibly will recognize that they have elements in their imagination that are intensified in Macbeth. I think that many of us fear that we have acted on our darkest impulses before we have fully apprehended them. There is something preternatu-

1

ral in Macbeth. He alone in his drama is in touch with the night world of Hecate and the Weird Sisters. I will soon be eighty-eight and find myself sometimes seeing and hearing things that are not there. This does not cause alarm because it stays on the border of actual hallucinations. But Macbeth has gone across that border. For him nothing is but what is not.

The play begins with the witches entering with thunder and lightning. We see them only briefly. They chant in riddles that are antithetical:

When the battle's lost and won.

act 1, scene 1, line 4

Fair is foul, and foul is fair.

act 1, scene 1, line 9

Our first account of Macbeth conveys his astonishing ferocity:

For brave Macbeth (well he deserves that name),
Disdaining Fortune, with his brandished steel,
Which smoked with bloody execution,
Like Valour's minion, carved out his passage,
Till he faced the slave,
Which ne'er shook hands, nor bade farewell to him,
Till he unseamed him from the nave to th' chops,
And fixed his head upon our battlements.

act 1, scene 2, lines 16–23

Slicing your opponent open from crotch to jaw is characteristic of Macbeth, who is described as the husband of the war goddess, or "Bellona's bridegroom." After Duncan, the Scottish king, adds the title of Thane of Cawdor to Macbeth's honors, we return to the three Witches. They accost Macbeth and his fellow captain Banquo:

Macbeth: So foul and fair a day I have not seen.
Banquo: How far is't call'd to Forres? What are these,
So withered and so wild in their attire,
That look not like th'inhabitants o'th' earth,
And yet are on't? Live you, or are you aught
That man may question? You seem to understand me,
By each at once her choppy finger laying
Upon her skinny lips. You should be women,
And yet your beards forbid me to interpret
That you are so.
Macbeth: Speak if you can: what are you?
1 Witch: All hail Macbeth, hail to thee, Thane of Glamis.
2 Witch: All hail Macbeth, hail to thee, Thane of Cawdor.
3 Witch: All hail Macbeth, that shalt be king hereafter.
Banquo: Good sir, why do you start, and seem to fear
Things that do sound so fair?—I'th' name of truth,
Are ye fantastical, or that indeed
Which outwardly ye show? My noble partner
You greet with present grace, and great prediction
Of noble having and of royal hope,
That he seems rapt withal. To me you speak not.

If you can look into the seeds of time,

And say which grain will grow, and which will not,

Speak then to me, who neither beg nor fear

Your favors nor your hate.

1 Witch: Hail.

2 Witch: Hail.

3 Witch: Hail.

1 Witch: Lesser than Macbeth, and greater.

2 Witch: Not so happy, yet much happier.

3 Witch: Thou shalt get kings, though thou be none:

So all hail, Macbeth, and Banquo.

1 Witch: Banquo, and Macbeth, all hail.

Macbeth: Stay, you imperfect speakers, tell me more.

By Finel's death, I know I am Thane of Glamis,

But how of Cawdor? The Thane of Cawdor lives

A prosperous gentleman: and to be king

Stands not within the prospect of belief,

No more than to be Cawdor. Say from whence

You owe this strange intelligence, or why

Upon this blasted heath you stop our way

With such prophetic greeting? Speak, I charge you.

Witches vanish.

act 1, scene 3, lines 38–78

Macbeth was played before King James I, who began as King James VI of Scotland. By tradition, James I was descended from Banquo. In Shakespeare's sources, Banquo was as guilty as Macbeth, but here he is stalwart and heroic. Finel was Macbeth's father,

while Banquo and Macbeth do not yet know of Cawdor's treach-ery. An extraordinary aside marks the advent of Macbeth's prolep-tic imagination:

Macbeth: [*aside*]   Two truths are told
As happy prologues to the swelling act
Of the imperial theme.—I thank you, gentlemen.—
This supernatural soliciting
Cannot be ill; cannot be good. If ill,
Why hath it given me earnest of success,
Commencing in a truth? I am Thane of Cawdor.
If good, why do I yield to that suggestion
Whose horrid image doth unfix my hair,
And make my seated heart knock at my ribs,
Against the use of nature? Present fears
Are less than horrible imaginings.
My thought, whose murder yet is but fantastical,
Shakes so my single state of man
That function is smothered in surmise,
And nothing is, but what is not.

                    act 1, scene 3, lines 129–44

The tormented grammar partly suggests Macbeth's psychic tur-moil. His murderous thought, though still a fantasy, so agitates his unaided state of man that function, or potential action, is smoth-ered in surmise, or censored by imagination.

The motto of Macbeth, both play and person, could well be: "And nothing is, but what is not." "Nothing" is used sixteen times in *Macbeth*. It is startling for me to realize that those sixteen occurrences are outweighed by thirty-four in *King Lear*, thirty-one in *Hamlet*, and twenty-six in *Othello*. But then, *Macbeth* is a ruthlessly economical tragedy of just over two thousand lines. The prominence of "nothing" in it is as salient as is the undersong of nothingness in the other three great tragedies of blood.

CHAPTER 2

False Face Must Hide
What the False Heart
Doth Know

Lady Macbeth is introduced to us as she reads aloud her husband's letter concerning the prophecies of the Weird Sisters. Her reaction sets the tone for her fierce nature:

> Glamis thou art, and Cawdor, and shalt be
> What thou art promised. Yet do I fear thy nature,
> It is too full o'th' milk of human kindness
> To catch the nearest way. Thou wouldst be great,
> Art not without ambition, but without
> The illness should attend it. What thou wouldst highly,
> That wouldst thou holily; wouldst not play false,
> And yet wouldst wrongly win. Thou'dst have, great Glamis,
> That which cries, 'Thus thou must do,' if thou have it;
> And that which rather thou dost fear to do,
> Than wishest should be undone. Hie thee hither,
> That I may pour my spirits in thine ear,

And chastise with the valour of my tongue
All that impedes thee from the golden round,
Which fate and metaphysical aid doth seem
To have thee crowned withal.

act 1, scene 5, lines 15–30

The now proverbial "milk of human kindness" requires a sense of the language of the English Renaissance. "Human" means "humane" and "kindness" probably means "kinship." "Illness" is "wickedness," while to pour spirits in the ear is to poison, as when the Ghost in *Hamlet* tells the Prince that Claudius, "in porches of my ear did pour / The leperous distilment," or when Iago plans to undo Othello: "I'll pour this pestilence into his ear."

"The golden round" is the crown of Scotland. Long ago I remember characterizing the Macbeths as the happiest marriage in Shakespeare. That can seem a grim jest, yet it is veracious. Their passion for each other is absolute in every way, as much metaphysical as erotic. The lust for power fuses with mutual desire and enhances the turbulence of their ecstasy.

Though Macbeth is a kinsman of the benign King Duncan, Lady Macbeth is of higher status. Shakespeare based her on Gruoch ingen Boite, the daughter of Boite mac Cináeda, son of Cináed III, King of Scots, known to the English as Kenneth III. Before she married Macbeth, Gruoch had been the wife of the King of Moray, to whom she bore a son, later King of Scots. Moray was burned alive by his enemies. Shakespeare implies that Gruoch's son died with his father.

"How many children had Lady Macbeth?" That was once a taunt indicting critics for regarding Shakespeare's personalities as real people. I regard the question as valid and useful. The answer seems to be at least one, though none with Macbeth. Their childlessness is one of Macbeth's obsessions. He sets himself to murder the future, but his hireling thugs fail to kill Fleance, the son of Banquo, though they do slaughter Banquo, Macbeth's comrade in arms. Fleance will be the ancestor of the Stuart kings of Scotland and then of England. As Macbeth's bloodlust heightens, he orders and is gratified by the massacre of Lady Macduff and all her children.

There are verbal hints throughout the play that Macbeth's ardor is so intense that he climaxes too soon each time he carnally embraces his wife. This seems related to the proleptic anxiety that governs his modes of thought and action. He over-anticipates and leaps too quickly to the other side of his intent. This may well account for the childlessness of the Macbeths. Lust in action is thwarted when it burns with furious intensity. Shakespeare is a great master of ellipses, of leaving things out. He relies upon our mature imaginations to fill out what is only suggested.

When Lady Macbeth is told that King Duncan will be her guest, she welcomes the news with a savage exaltation:

> The raven himself is hoarse
> That croaks the fatal entrance of Duncan
> Under my battlements. Come you spirits
> That tend on mortal thoughts, unsex me here,
> And fill me from the crown to the toe, top-ful

Of direst cruelty. Make thick my blood,

Stop up th'access and passage to remorse,

That no compunctious visitings of nature

Shake my fell purpose, nor keep peace between

Th'effect and it. Come to my woman's breasts,

And take my milk for gall, you murdering ministers,

Wherever in your sightless substances

You wait on nature's mischief. Come thick night,

And pall thee in the dunnest smoke of hell,

That my keen knife see not the wound it makes,

Nor heaven peep through the blanket of the dark

To cry, 'Hold, hold.'

act 1, scene 5, lines 38–54

I attended an Old Vic *Macbeth* in London, 1954, in which Paul Rogers played Macbeth and Ann Todd his Lady. I found Ann Todd's performance profoundly disturbing. Michael Benthall, the director, had her double over, holding her vulva, as she cried out "unsex me here." Red-headed and brandishing a rapier, her image burned onto my memory, so that now it returns to me each time I reread and teach *Macbeth*.

Lady Macbeth's sway over her husband manifests at the first moment we see them together:

Enter Macbeth.

Lady Macbeth: Great Glamis, worthy Cawdor,

Greater than both, by the all-hail hereafter,

Thy letters have transported me beyond

This ignorant present, and I feel now
The future in the instant.
Macbeth: My dearest love,
Duncan comes here tonight.
Lady Macbeth: And when goes hence?
Macbeth: Tomorrow, as he purposes.
Lady Macbeth: O never
Shall sun that morrow see.
Your face, my thane, is as a book, where men
May read strange matters; to beguile the time,
Look like the time, bear welcome in your eye,
Your hand, your tongue; look like the innocent flower,
But be the serpent under't. He that's coming
Must be provided for; and you shall put
This night's great business into my dispatch,
Which shall to all our nights and days to come
Give solely sovereign sway and masterdom.
Macbeth: We will speak further.
Lady Macbeth: Only look up clear;
To alter favour ever is to fear.
Leave all the rest to me.   *Exeunt.*

                     act 1, scene 5, lines 54–73

In a drama of just two thousand lines, "time" is employed in fifty-one instances. "All-hail hereafter!" echoes the "hereafter" of the third Witch, though it is not clear if it is a part of Macbeth's letter. Though Lady Macbeth does not share her husband's proleptic affliction, she seems influenced by it:

Thy letters have transported me beyond

This ignorant present, and I feel now

The future in the instant.

When she advises him: "to beguile the time, / Look like the time," she again is contaminated by his spirit. A pleasant diversion becomes the mask of the future. The management she proposes for herself in "my dispatch" implies also the murder of Duncan. As the daughter of a king, she finds her authentic voice in "Give solely sovereign sway and masterdom" and in the confident "Leave all the rest to me."

To the music of hautboys and by torchlight, King Duncan and his entourage behold Macbeth's castle. Both Duncan and Banquo activate our sense of dread by their innocence as they enter their destruction:

Duncan: This castle hath a pleasant seat, the air

Nimbly and sweetly recommends itself

Unto our gentle senses.

Banquo:　　　　　　　This guest of summer,

The temple-haunting martlet, does approve,

By his loved mansionry, that the heaven's breath

Smells wooingly here. No jutty frieze,

Buttress, nor coin of vantage, but this bird

Hath made his pendant bed and procreant cradle:

Where they must breed and haunt, I have observed

The air is delicate.

act 1, scene 6, lines 1–10

The martlet is a swift or swallow, whose nest adheres to walls, and was regarded as lucky.

Enter Lady Macbeth.

Duncan: See, see, our honoured hostess.
The love that follows us sometime is our trouble,
Which still we thank as love. Herein I teach you
How you shall bid God yield us for your pains,
And thank us for your trouble.

Lady Macbeth: All our service
In every point twice done, and then done double,
Were poor and single business to contend
Against those honours deep and broad wherewith
Your Majesty loads our house. For those of old,
And the late dignities heaped up to them,
We rest your hermits.

Duncan: Where's the Thane of Cawdor?
We coursed him at the heels, and had a purpose
To be his purveyor. But he rides well,
And his great love, sharp as his spur, hath holp him
To his home before us. Fair and noble hostess,
We are your guest tonight.

Lady Macbeth: Your servants ever,
Have theirs, themselves, and what is theirs in count,
To make their audit at your highness' pleasure,
Still to return your own.

Duncan: Give me your hand.
Conduct me to mine host: we love him highly,

13

And shall continue our graces towards him.

By your leave, hostess.   *Exeunt.*

act 1, scene 6, lines 10–31

There is a strange cruelty in this exchange. Duncan, a lowlander, has little sense of the barbaric Highlands of the Macbeths. Lady Macbeth's graciousness scarcely conceals her impending savagery. Suddenly we see Macbeth, alone onstage for the first time, and listen to his astonishing soliloquy, in which his involuntary prophetic gift breaks in upon him:

If it were done, when 'tis done, then 'twere well

It were done quickly. If th'assassination

Could trammel up the consequence, and catch

With his surcease, success: that but this blow

Might be the be-all and the end-all, here,

But here, upon this bank and shoal of time,

We'd jump the life to come.

act 1, scene 7, lines 1–7

When I reread this, I hear Ian McKellen superbly handling the hissing sibilants and the rolling "r"s of "were" and "here." The triple "done" is ambiguous. Does it mean performed or ended? "Assassination" may have been a Shakespearean coinage. To "trammel up" is to entangle, whether netting fish or hobbling a horse. The wordplay of "surcease, success" is intricate. Presumably the death of Duncan would be surcease, yet success might mean Macbeth's hoped-for successors or simply what will happen next.

The play of "be-all and the end-all" is another Shakespearean invention. The "bank and shoal" is an emendation, which I am reluctant to accept. Shakespeare's word is "schoole" and "this bank" is probably a bench.

> But in these cases,
> We still have judgement here, that we but teach
> Bloody instructions, which being taught, return
> To plague th'inventor. This even-handed justice
> Commends th'ingredience of our poisoned chalice
> To our own lips. He's here in double trust:
> First, as I am his kinsman, and his subject,
> Strong both against the deed. Then, as his host,
> Who should against his murderer shut the door,
> Not bear the knife myself. Besides, this Duncan
> Hath borne his faculties so meek, hath been
> So clear in his great office, that his virtues
> Will plead like angels, trumpet-tongued, against
> The deep damnation of his taking-off;
> And pity, like a naked new-born babe,
> Striding the blast, or heaven's cherubin, horsed
> Upon the sightless couriers of the air,
> Shall blow the horrid deed in every eye,
> That tears shall drown the wind. I have no spur
> To prick the sides of my intent, but only
> Vaulting ambition, which o'er-leaps itself,
> And falls on th'other.

act 1, scene 7, lines 7–28

15

Leaping over life after death, Macbeth anticipates a judgment against himself. Justice, even-handed, may put him in the situation of the shuffling Claudius, forced by Hamlet to drink the poisoned chalice that ended Gertrude, and was meant for Hamlet. A great voice breaks in upon Macbeth, trumpeting the angelic nature of Duncan, and announcing the descent of pity, in the guise of a naked newborn babe, riding the wind, or of the baby-like cherubim, horsed upon the invisible winds. Macbeth, overleaping the stallion of his will, vaults too high, and falls on the other side.

Lady Macbeth enters to argue her husband back to their mutual resolve:

> **Macbeth:** We will proceed no further in this business:
> He hath honoured me of late, and I have bought
> Golden opinions from all sorts of people,
> Which would be worn now in their newest gloss,
> Not cast aside so soon.
> **Lady Macbeth:**   Was the hope drunk
> Wherein you dressed yourself? Hath it slept since?
> And wakes it now to look so green and pale
> At what it did so freely? From this time
> Such I account thy love. Art thou afeared
> To be the same in thine own act and valour,
> As thou art in desire? Wouldst thou have that
> Which thou esteem'st the ornament of life,
> And live a coward in thine own esteem,
> Letting 'I dare not' wait upon 'I would,'

Like the poor cat i'th' adage?

act 1, scene 7, lines 31–45

Her disdain powerfully depicts Macbeth as a drunkard, who rises from besotted sleep, afflicted by the remorse of nausea. There is sexual reproach in her contempt, compounding ambition and lust, taunting him for inadequacy. For Lady Macbeth, the ornament of life is the crown. The proverbial adage of the cat, wanting to devour fish, but daring not get his feet wet, augments her goading.

Macbeth: Prithee peace.
I dare do all that may become a man,
Who dares do more, is none.
Lady Macbeth: What beast was't then
That made you break this enterprise to me?
When you durst do it, then you were a man;
And to be more than what you were, you would
Be so much more the man. Nor time nor place
Did then adhere, and yet you would make both:
They have made themselves, and that their fitness now
Does unmake you. I have given suck, and know
How tender 'tis to love the babe that milks me:
I would, while it was smiling in my face,
Have plucked my nipple from his boneless gums,
And dashed the brains out, had I so sworn
As you have done to this.

act 1, scene 7, lines 45–59

17

Again she questions his virility, implying that his retreat from daring unmans him. We wince at the image of dashing out the brains of her son whom she had previously lost, when he and her first husband were murdered.

Macbeth: If we should fail?
Lady Macbeth: We fail?
But screw your courage to the sticking place,
And we'll not fail.

act 1, scene 7, lines 59–62

This can be taken as an image for tightening a musical instrument, or winding up a crossbow's cord. Yet the sexual reproach is there again, as she urges Macbeth to stiffen his spirit to the utmost point.

>   When Duncan is asleep,
> Whereto the rather shall his day's hard journey
> Soundly invite him, his two chamberlains
> Will I with wine and wassail so convince,
> That memory, the warder of the brain,
> Shall be a fume, and the receipt of reason
> A limbeck only. When in swinish sleep
> Their drenched natures lies as in a death,
> What cannot you and I perform upon
> Th'unguarded Duncan? What not put upon
> His spongy officers, who shall bear the guilt
> Of our great quell?

Macbeth: Bring forth men-children only;
For thy undaunted mettle should compose
Nothing but males. Will it not be received,
When we have marked with blood those sleepy two
Of his own chamber, and used their very daggers,
That they have done't?
Lady Macbeth: Who dares receive it other,
As we shall make our griefs and clamour roar
Upon his death?
Macbeth: I am settled, and bend up
Each corporal agent to this terrible feat.
Away, and mock the time with fairest show:
False face must hide what the false heart doth know.

                    act 1, scene 7, lines 62–83

Macbeth's resolution is overtly phallic in its continuation of the metaphor of tightening either an instrument or a crossbow. Yet the irony is that you cannot mock the time; it will mock you. The monosyllabic final line fuses the falsity of heart and face in this distortion of knowing.

CHAPTER 3

A Dagger of the Mind, a False Creation

A troubled Banquo enters, with his son Fleance, and remarks upon the darkness of the night:

> **Banquo:** Hold, take my sword. There's husbandry in heaven,
> Their candles are all out; take thee that too.
> A heavy summons lies like lead upon me,
> And yet I would not sleep. Merciful powers,
> Restrain in me the cursed thoughts that nature
> Gives way to in repose.
> > *Enter Macbeth, and a Servant with a torch.*
> Give me my sword; who's there?
> **Macbeth:** A friend.
> > act 2, scene 1, lines 4–11

The husbandry or thrift of heaven has blown out the candles of starlight. Banquo is afflicted by memories of the Weird Sisters, and by his own sense of foreboding. A curious exchange with Macbeth manifests the common uneasiness of the two warriors. Tentatively

Macbeth sounds out Banquo's loyalty to Duncan, and receives a firm reply:

Banquo: So I lose none
In seeking to augment it, but still keep
My bosom franchised and allegiance clear,
I shall be counselled.

                                        act 2, scene 1, lines 26–29

When Banquo departs, Macbeth suffers a hallucinatory soliloquy:

Is this a dagger which I see before me,
The handle toward my hand? Come, let me clutch thee.
I have thee not, and yet I see thee still.
Art thou not, fatal vision, sensible
To feeling as to sight? Or art thou but
A dagger of the mind, a false creation,
Proceeding from the heat-oppressed brain?

                                        act 2, scene 1, lines 33–39

Ancient heresies spoke of a demiurge fevering to a false creation. Weird Macbeth increasingly harbors such a demiurge. The ominous or fatal vision partly veils itself.

I see thee yet, in form as palpable
As this which now I draw.
Thou marshall'st me the way that I was going,
And such an instrument I was to use.

Mine eyes are made the fools o'th' other senses,
Or else worth all the rest. I see thee still,
And on thy blade and dudgeon, gouts of blood,
Which was not so before.

act 2, scene 1, lines 40–47

The hilt of the dagger, the dudgeon with its Scottish aura, and
the dagger itself, receive impetus from Macbeth's will. Yet he cannot control his own imaginative thrust. The splashes of blood are
purely visionary, and Macbeth knows it.

There's no such thing.
It is the bloody business which informs
Thus to mine eyes. Now o'er the one half-world
Nature seems dead, and wicked dreams abuse
The curtained sleep; Witchcraft celebrates
Pale Hecate's offerings; and withered Murder,
Alarumed by his sentinel, the wolf,
Whose howl's his watch, thus with his stealthy pace,
With Tarquin's ravishing strides, towards his design
Moves like a ghost.

act 2, scene 1, lines 47–56

Nature sleeps, and the preternatural usurps it. Hecate, pale moon
goddess, presides over all sorcery. The howl of a wolf alerts the
withered old man—a personification of Murder quite uncharac-
teristic of Shakespeare—that action impends. Shakespeare echoes
his poem *Lucrece* (1594) when Macbeth identifies with the Roman

tyrant, whose rape of the noble matron Lucrece leads to her suicide, and subsequently to his own overthrow. "Ravishing *strides*" is Alexander Pope's emendation, but I prefer the Folio's "*sides*."

> Thou sure and firm-set earth,
> Hear not my steps, which way they walk, for fear
> The very stones prate of my whereabout,
> And take the present horror from the time,
> Which now suits with it. Whiles I threat, he lives:
> Words to the heat of deeds too cold breath gives.   *A bell rings.*
> I go, and it is done; the bell invites me.
> Hear it not, Duncan, for it is a knell,
> That summons thee to heaven, or to hell.
>
> act 2, scene 1, lines 56–64

As the bell rings, Macbeth again leaps into the future, and the butchery is already accomplished. Macbeth's imagination is itself a dagger of the mind. As Hamlet's tragedy is of the mind, Macbeth's is of the fantasy-making power. I play with the notion that Hamlet embodies more of Shakespeare's capacious consciousness than seems possible for a figure made up of words. A darker play makes me wonder whether Shakespeare has not endowed Macbeth with one crucial aspect of his own imagination, in which the poet-dramatist anticipates feeling all actions before they are formulated. We are distanced from Hamlet, but Macbeth becomes our own journey into the interior. Can we avoid being complicit with him?

Hamlet's theatricalism and his inwardness at last part company when he returns to Denmark from the sea. Macbeth is a poor player, always missing his cue. We cannot say that Hamlet is one of the fools of time. Macbeth, more even than Iago and Edmund, lives for crime and dies by misreading the auguries. No one, except Lady Macbeth, loves him, but why are we so intimate with his aspirations? Is it because he opens us to the night world? Many among us have seen strange things that ought not to have been there. In Edinburgh, during the summer I turned twenty-one, I distinctly saw a ghost wandering the mazelike garden of the Carlyle Hostel, at 3:00 a.m. in the murky fog. Two-thirds of a century later, I can still see that uncanny bundle of rags coming by me as I turned in the labyrinth. The grand Scottish lady who administered the hostel told me the next morning of a seventeenth-century cleaning woman who had been murdered there.

Meditating again upon Macbeth, I begin to believe he represents an element buried in many among us. Call it the impulse to murder time and outwardness. We are not warriors and lack his tolerance for blood. But why is it that Shakespeare will not show him dying upon the stage? When Macduff enters with Macbeth's head, we are released yet do not rejoice. A murderous imagination that powerful diminishes us when it is obliterated.

William Blake's Proverb of Hell "Exuberance is Beauty" could be the motto of *The Tragedie of Macbeth*. The energy of sheer being in the Macbeths captivates us. However negative their zest, it remains sublime. Even a wicked transcendence assaults the heavens and thrusts our horizons upward and outward.

Lady Macbeth, heightened both by enterprise and by wine, stimulates us with a brief soliloquy as she enters:

That which hath made them drunk, hath made me bold;
What hath quenched them hath given me fire.
Hark, peace; it was the owl that shrieked,
The fatal bellman, which gives the stern'st good-night.
He is about it. The doors are open
And the surfeited grooms do mock their charge
With snores. I have drugged their possets
That death and nature do contend about them,
Whether they live or die.

act 2, scene 2, lines 1–9

The wretched grooms are quenched by wine, but Lady Macbeth is enkindled. The shriek of the owl is a dark omen, and the town crier or bellman is fatal, presaging death. "He is about it" is a dry description of Macbeth's murder of Duncan. The Lady has poisoned the wine imbibed by the grooms, who hover between life and death.

With Macbeth's entrance, dialogue takes on a nervous edge, more acute than elsewhere in Shakespeare:

Macbeth: Who's there? What ho?
Lady Macbeth: Alack, I am afraid they have awaked,
And 'tis not done. The attempt, and not the deed
Confounds us. Hark. I laid their daggers ready;
He could not miss 'em. Had he not resembled
My father as he slept, I had done't.
My husband?

act 2, scene 2, lines 9–15

This fierce virago touches her limit at parricide. The scene is so dark as to make her uncertain of Macbeth's identity. This is the only time she employs the word "husband." The crickets are familiars of the witches.

Macbeth: I have done the deed.
Didst thou not hear a noise?
Lady Macbeth: I heard the owl scream and the crickets cry.
Did not you speak?
Macbeth: When?
Lady Macbeth: Now.
Macbeth: As I descended?
Lady Macbeth: Ay.
Macbeth: Hark, who lies i'the second chamber?
Lady Macbeth: Donalbain.
Macbeth: This is a sorry sight.
Lady Macbeth: A foolish thought, to say a sorry sight.
Macbeth: There's one did laugh in 's sleep,
And one cried, 'Murder,' that they did wake each other.
I stood and heard them; but they did say their prayers
And addressed them again to sleep.
Lady Macbeth: There are two lodged together.
Macbeth: One cried, 'God bless us,' and 'Amen' the other,
As they had seen me with these hangman's hands.
Listening their fear, I could not say 'Amen'
When they did say, 'God bless us.'
Lady Macbeth: Consider it not so deeply.
Macbeth: But wherefore could not I pronounce 'Amen'?

I had most need of blessing, and 'Amen'
Stuck in my throat.
Lady Macbeth:　　　These deeds must not be thought
After these ways; so, it will make us mad.

act 2, scene 2, lines 15–35

She is prophetic and indeed will go mad, yet he will not. It fascinates me that she is the stronger of the two in will and audacity, yet the cost of that will gradually diminishes her. Macbeth, virtually useless in this aftermath, will recover and surge on from enormity to enormity.

Macbeth: Methought I heard a voice cry, 'Sleep no more.
Macbeth does murder sleep'—the innocent sleep,
Sleep that knits up the ravelled sleave of care,
The death of each day's life, sore labour's bath,
Balm of hurt minds, great Nature's second course,
Chief nourisher in life's feast—
Lady Macbeth:　　　　　What do you mean?
Macbeth: Still it cried, 'Sleep no more' to all the house;
'Glamis hath murdered sleep, and therefore Cawdor
Shall sleep no more. Macbeth shall sleep no more.'
Lady Macbeth: Who was it that thus cried?

act 2, scene 2, lines 36–45

A voice greater than Macbeth's descends on him, and identifies the sleeping Duncan with sleep itself. Lady Macbeth cannot hear it, but Shakespeare insists that we can. We are Macbeth. It is a dark irony that she, not he, will be "brainsickly."

Lady Macbeth: Why, worthy thane,
You do unbend your noble strength, to think
So brainsickly of things. Go, get some water
And wash this filthy witness from your hand.
Why did you bring these daggers from the place?
They must lie there. Go carry them, and smear
The sleepy grooms with blood.
Macbeth: I'll go no more.
I am afraid to think what I have done;
Look on't again, I dare not.
Lady Macbeth: Infirm of purpose,
Give me the daggers. The sleeping and the dead
Are but as pictures; 'tis the eye of childhood
That fears a painted devil. If he do bleed,
I'll gild the faces of the grooms withal,
For it must seem their guilt.   *Exit. Knock within.*

                    act 2, scene 2, lines 45–58

The wordplay on "gild" and "guilt" turns on the redness of old gold, and strengthens our sense of Lady Macbeth's frightening control of her own revulsion. The knocking at the gate continues throughout this and the next scene. The English essayist Thomas De Quincey in his "On the Knocking at the Gate in *Macbeth*" (1823) gave us the classical commentary on this:

The knocking at the gate is heard; and it makes known audibly that the reaction has commenced: the human has made its reflux upon the fiendish; the pulses of life are beginning to beat again; and the re-establishment of the goings-on of the world in which we live, first makes us profoundly sensible of the awful parenthesis that had suspended them.

Macbeth reacts obsessively to the knocking:

> Whence is that knocking?
> How is't with me, when every noise appals me?
> What hands are here? Ha: they pluck out mine eyes.
> Will all great Neptune's ocean wash this blood
> Clean from my hand? No, this my hand will rather
> The multitudinous seas incarnadine,
> Making the green one red.
>
> act 2, scene 2, lines 58–64

Macbeth's eloquence is grand and frightening. His own bloody hands momentarily seem to emanate from his blinded eyes, perhaps echoing the plucking out of Gloucester's eyes by Cornwall in *King Lear*. Shakespeare invents "incarnadine" as a verb, and pairs it with "multitudinous," a coinage shared with Ben Jonson. The blood-dimmed tide is reddened on an enormous scale.

Lady Macbeth re-enters and again outdoes her husband in constancy:

Lady Macbeth: My hands are of your colour, but I shame
To wear a heart so white. I hear a knocking   *Knock*
At the south entry. Retire we to our chamber;
A little water clears us of this deed.
How easy is it then. Your constancy
Hath left you unattended.   *Knock*
                              Hark, more knocking.
Get on your nightgown, lest occasion call us
And show us to be watchers. Be not lost
So poorly in your thoughts.
Macbeth: To know my deed, 'twere best not know myself.   *Knock*
Wake Duncan with thy knocking. I would thou couldst!

                                        Exeunt.

                    act 2, scene 2, lines 65–75

Her hands are bloody, yet her heart is white, not from fear but manifesting amazing innocence. We shudder at the ease of a cleansing and again at her accusation that her husband is unmanned. The knocking continues while a curious detachment from self overcomes Macbeth. He seems to himself a false creation, a dagger of the mind.

CHAPTER 4

In the Great Hand
of God I Stand

The wonderful ironies of the Porter are antiphonal to the incessant knocking at the gate. Macduff and Lennox have come to greet Duncan, but they confront a Shakespearean clown so memorable that he challenges Lear's Fool:

> Here's a knocking indeed: If a man were porter of Hell Gate,
> he should have old turning the key.

In a sense he is the porter of Hell Gate, and "should have old" means he admits many to perdition.

> (*Knock*) Knock, knock, knock. Who's there, i'th' name of
> Belzebub?

Belzebub, prince of devils, is accurately invoked.

> Here's a farmer, that hanged himself on th'expectation of
> plenty.

The corrupt farmer hangs himself, since he hoped to extort outrageous prices in a bad harvest and could not survive the expectation of plenty. Yet there is a dark enrichment in this image, since Father Henry Garnet was known by the code name "Farmer." I am a little wary of turning the drama *Macbeth* into a treatise on the Gunpowder Plot of 1605, as Garry Wills does in his lively *Witches and Jesuits: Shakespeare's* Macbeth (1995). Yet the rich verb "equivocate" indeed is crucial and requires some contextualization. The Jesuit Garnet had written a *Treatise of Equivocation* in 1598, defending the doctrine of mental reservation, which allowed a Roman Catholic undergoing legal questioning to hold back part of an incriminating testimony, or to speak ambiguously, so long as in his heart he affirmed truth. Garnet had urged Robert Catesby, chief conspirator of the Gunpowder Plot, to forsake violence. Nevertheless, since Catesby's revelation came through the act of confession, Garnet did not divulge the information. Questioned by the Privy Council, Garnet equivocated and was executed horribly by hanging, drawing, and quartering.

> Come in time. Have napkins enow about you; here you'll
> sweat for't. (*Knock*) Knock, knock. Who's there, in th'other
> devil's name? Faith, here's an equivocator that could swear in
> both the scales against either scale, who committed treason
> enough for God's sake, yet could not equivocate to heaven.
> O, come in, equivocator. (*Knock*) Knock, knock, knock. Who's
> there? Faith, here's an English tailor come hither, for stealing
> out of a French hose. Come in, tailor; here you may roast your

goose. (*Knock*) Knock, knock. Never at quiet! What are you?
But this place is too cold for hell. I'll devil-porter it no further.
I had thought to have let in some of all professions that go the
primrose way to the everlasting bonfire. (*Knock*) Anon, anon, I
pray you, remember the porter.

act 2, scene 3, lines 1–20

The Porter delights me. Drunk and exuberant, he urges all who
enter to have enough napkins or handkerchiefs, since hell-fire will
sweat them. The other devil presumably is Lucifer. English tailors
were notorious for stealing by skimping on cloth, making breeches
or French hose inadequate. Roasting your goose was slang for
enjoying a whore. We are not likely to forget the Porter, but he is
probably asking Macduff and Lennox for a tip:

Enter Macduff and Lennox.
Macduff: Was it so late, friend, ere you went to bed,
That you do lie so late?
Porter: Faith, sir, we were carousing till the second cock; and
drink, sir, is a great provoker of three things.
Macduff: What three things does drink especially provoke?
Porter: Marry, sir, nose-painting, sleep and urine. Lechery, sir,
it provokes and unprovokes: it provokes the desire, but it takes
away the performance. Therefore much drink may be said to
be an equivocator with lechery: it makes him, and it mars
him; it sets him on, and it takes him off; it persuades him,
and disheartens him; makes him stand to, and not stand to; in

conclusion, equivocates him in a sleep and, giving him the lie, leaves him.

act 2, scene 3, lines 21–35

This low humor is effective enough but is raised to disturbing intensity by the return of "equivocator" and "equivocates."

Macduff: I believe drink gave thee the lie last night.
Porter: That it did, sir, i'the very throat on me; but I requited him for his lie, and, I think, being too strong for him, though he took up my legs sometime, yet I made a shift to cast him.

act 2, scene 3, lines 36–40

The outrage of lying is fit prelude to the equivocation of Macbeth's "Not yet":

Macduff: Is thy master stirring?
Our knocking has awaked him; here he comes. *Exit Porter.*
Enter Macbeth.
Lennox: Good morrow, noble sir.
Macbeth: Good morrow both.
Macduff: Is the King stirring, worthy thane?
Macbeth: Not yet.
Macduff: He did command me to call timely on him;
I have almost slipped the hour.
Macbeth: I'll bring you to him.
Macduff: I know this is a joyful trouble to you;
But yet 'tis one.

Macbeth: The labour we delight in physics pain;
This is the door.
Macduff: I'll make so bold to call, for 'tis my limited service.

Exit Macduff.

Lennox: Goes the King hence today?
Macbeth: He does: he did appoint so.
Lennox: The night has been unruly: where we lay
Our chimneys were blown down and, as they say,
Lamentings heard i'th' air, strange screams of death,
And prophesying, with accents terrible,
Of dire combustion, and confused events
New hatched to th' woeful time. The obscure bird
Clamoured the livelong night. Some say the earth
Was feverous and did shake.

act 2, scene 3, lines 41–61

The "obscure bird" is the owl prophesying fiery destruction, and the fevered earthquakes.

Macbeth: 'Twas a rough night.
Lennox: My young remembrance cannot parallel
A fellow to it.

Macduff bursts in and proclaims the horror:

Macduff: O horror, horror, horror.
Tongue nor heart cannot conceive nor name thee.
Macbeth and Lennox: What's the matter?

Macduff: Confusion now hath made his masterpiece.

Most sacrilegious murder hath broke ope

The Lord's anointed temple, and stole thence

The life o'th' building.

Macbeth: What is't you say? the life?

Lennox: Mean you his majesty?

Macduff: Approach the chamber, and destroy your sight

With a new Gorgon.

act 2, scene 3, lines 61–72

The Gorgons were three dreadful sisters, Stheno, Euryale, and Medusa, all with snakes for hair, who turned any gazer to stone.

Macduff: Do not bid me speak—

See, and then speak yourselves.

Exeunt Macbeth and Lennox.

Awake, awake!

Ring the alarum bell! Murder and treason.

Banquo and Donalbain, Malcolm, awake,

Shake off this downy sleep, death's counterfeit,

And look on death itself. Up, up, and see

The great doom's image. Malcolm, Banquo,

As from your graves rise up, and walk like sprites

To countenance this horror. Ring the bell! *Bell rings.*

act 2, scene 3, lines 72–80

As the bell tolls, Macduff summons the King's sons and Banquo to behold an image of the Last Judgment. In keeping with this dread finality, they are urged to rise like the resurrected dead. Instead Lady Macbeth rises:

> **Lady Macbeth:** What's the business,
> That such a hideous trumpet calls to parley
> The sleepers of the house? Speak, speak.
>
> act 2, scene 3, lines 81–83

The trumpet is the alarm bell yet alludes to the trumpet of the Last Judgment:

> **51** Behold, I show you a secret thing, We shall not all sleep, but we shall all be changed,
> **52** In a moment, in the twinkling of an eye at the last trumpet: for the trumpet shall blow, and the dead shall be raised up incorruptible, and we shall be changed.
>
> 1 Corinthians 15:51–52, Geneva Bible

> **Macduff:** O gentle lady,
> 'Tis not for you to hear what I can speak:
> The repetition in a woman's ear
> Would murder as it fell.
> *Enter Banquo.*
>   O Banquo, Banquo,
> Our royal master's murdered!
> **Lady Macbeth:**   Woe, alas.
> What, in our house?

Banquo: Too cruel anywhere.

Dear Duff, I prithee contradict thyself

And say it is not so.

Enter Macbeth, Lennox, and Ross.

Macbeth: Had I but died an hour before this chance,

I had lived a blessed time; for from this instant

There's nothing serious in mortality;

All is but toys; renown and grace is dead,

The wine of life is drawn, and the mere lees

Is left this vault to brag of.

act 2, scene 3, lines 84–97

I've always been fascinated by this declaration of Macbeth's. There is deception in it, yet even that deception yields to sincere lament. Macbeth himself has slain renown and grace and rendered the human condition, mortality, to so many toys. The vault of the heavens can boast only what is left behind when the wine of life has been consumed.

The King's sons enter to learn their sorrow:

Donalbain: What is amiss?

Macbeth: You are, and do not know't:

The spring, the head, the fountain of your blood

Is stopped, the very source of it is stopped.

Macduff: Your royal father's murdered.

Malcolm: O, by whom?

Lennox: Those of his chamber, as it seemed, had done't.

Their hands and faces were all badged with blood;

So were their daggers, which unwiped we found

Upon their pillows. They stared, and were distracted;

No man's life was to be trusted with them.

Macbeth: O, yet I do repent me of my fury,

That I did kill them.

Macduff: Wherefore did you so?

Macbeth: Who can be wise, amazed, temperate and furious,

Loyal and neutral, in a moment? No man.

The expedition of my violent love

Outrun the pauser, reason. Here lay Duncan,

His silver skin laced with his golden blood,

And his gashed stabs looked like a breach in nature

For ruin's wasteful entrance; there, the murderers,

Steeped in the colours of their trade, their daggers

Unmannerly breeched with gore. Who could refrain,

That had a heart to love, and in that heart

Courage to make's love known?

act 2, scene 3, lines 97–119

Macbeth's eloquence, though misplaced, remains extraordinary. He is the poet of the dagger. The vision of Duncan has a perilous aesthetic, of white skin viewed as silver and laced with the red gold of blood.

Lady Macbeth, whether it be real or simulated, has a fainting fit, prompting both Macduff and Banquo to cry, "Look to the lady."

She is led away from a turbulent scene, in which Malcolm and Donalbain, Duncan's sons, resolve to depart, and the thanes vow their steadfastness:

> **Malcolm:** Why do we hold our tongues, that most may claim
> This argument for ours?
> **Donalbain:**   What should be spoken
> Here, where our fate, hid in an auger hole,
> May rush and seize us?

"Hid in an auger hole" is to be concealed in a small space, a hole bored by an auger.

> **Donalbain:**   Let's away,
> Our tears are not yet brewed.
> **Malcolm:**   Nor our strong sorrow
> Upon the foot of motion.
> **Banquo:**   Look to the lady.   *Exit Lady.*
> And when we have our naked frailties hid,
> That suffer in exposure, let us meet
> And question this most bloody piece of work
> To know it further. Fears and scruples shake us.
> In the great hand of God I stand, and thence
> Against the undivulged pretence I fight
> Of treasonous malice.
>
>   act 2, scene 3, lines 121–33

Banquo's powerful affirmation of his loyalty and innocence is expressed with vehemence and power: "In the great hand of God I stand." Yet that determines his fate, since Macbeth fears him, and is determined to destroy both father and son, Banquo and Fleance.

Macduff: And so do I.

All: So all.

Macbeth: Let's briefly put on manly readiness
And meet i'the hall together.

All: Well contented.

Exeunt all but Malcolm and Donalbain.

Malcolm: What will you do? Let's not consort with them.
To show an unfelt sorrow is an office
Which the false man does easy. I'll to England.

Donalbain: To Ireland, I; our separated fortune
Shall keep us both the safer. Where we are,
There's daggers in men's smiles; the near in blood,
The nearer bloody.

act 2, scene 3, lines 133–42

As we are nearest to Duncan in blood, the likelier our own blood soon will be sought. Shrewdly suspicious of Macbeth, the brothers depart unobserved. The future King Malcolm puns on the double meaning of "steals itself," at once flight and theft. Surrounded by murderous or at least equivocal thanes, Malcolm begins to show the resourcefulness of royalty:

Malcolm:　　　　　　This murderous shaft that's shot
Hath not yet lighted, and our safest way
Is to avoid the aim. Therefore to horse;
And let us not be dainty of leave-taking,
But shift away. There's warrant in that theft
Which steals itself, when there's no mercy left.

　　　　　　　　　　　act 2, scene 3, lines 142–47

I am always rather baffled when directors delete the following scene, since it is superbly relevant to Shakespeare's darker purpose:

Old Man: Threescore and ten I can remember well,
Within the volume of which time I have seen
Hours dreadful and things strange; but this sore night
Hath trifled former knowings.
Ross:　　　　　　　　　Ha, good father,
Thou seest the heavens, as troubled with man's act,
Threatens his bloody stage. By th' clock 'tis day,
And yet dark night strangles the travelling lamp.
Is't night's predominance, or the day's shame,
That darkness does the face of earth entomb
When living light should kiss it?
Old Man:　　　　　　　　　'Tis unnatural,
Even like the deed that's done. On Tuesday last
A falcon towering in her pride of place
Was by a mousing owl hawked at and killed.
Ross: And Duncan's horses, a thing most strange and certain,

Beauteous and swift, the minions of their race,
Turned wild in nature, broke their stalls, flung out
Contending 'gainst obedience, as they would
Make war with mankind.
Old Man: 'Tis said, they eat each other.
Ross: They did so, to th'amazement of mine eyes
That looked upon't.

act 2, scene 4, lines 1–20

The Old Man is unidentified and seems to have a capacity for vision. The sore or violent night has made earlier disturbances mere trifles. The Old Man has kindled Ross to clothe the event with the emblems of theater. The bloody stage of *Macbeth* is menaced as though the canopy above it is transmuted into the angry heavens. The Folio reads "travailing lamp," as though the sun despite its labors is strangled by darkness. The day's shame, murder of the King, buries earth as in a tomb, or the powerful influence of night does the same work. The aged oracle recalls the unnatural event of a high falcon attacked and slain by a low-flying owl. Prolonging the wonderment, Ross reports Duncan's horses, favorites of their breed, turning wild and breaking loose, in war upon mankind. The ultimate marvel is the Old Man's "'Tis said, they eat each other," and the confirmation by Ross, who observed it.

Abruptly, with the entrance of Macduff, the tragedy proceeds:

Ross: Here comes the good Macduff.
How goes the world, sir, now?

Macduff: Why, see you not?

Ross: Is't known who did this more than bloody deed?

Macduff: Those that Macbeth hath slain.

act 2, scene 4, lines 20–23

Macduff's words conceal his thoughts. Ultimate avenger, he doubts the guilt of Malcolm and Donalbain, and is laconic in his replies to Ross:

Ross: Alas, the day.
What good could they pretend?
Macduff: They were suborned.
Malcolm and Donalbain, the King's two sons,
Are stolen away and fled, which puts upon them
Suspicion of the deed.
Ross: 'Gainst nature still,
Thriftless ambition, that will raven up
Thine own life's means. Then 'tis most like
The sovereignty will fall upon Macbeth.

act 2, scene 4, lines 23–30

The credulous Ross accepts the guilt of the royal sons, whose ambition will raven or swallow up the means to sustain their own lives.

Macduff: He is already named, and gone to Scone
To be invested.
Ross: Where is Duncan's body?

Macduff: Carried to Colmekill,
The sacred store-house of his predecessors
And guardian of their bones.

act 2, scene 4, lines 31–35

Colmekill is the island of Iona, traditional resting place of the Scottish kings. Macduff, sagely avoiding the coronation at Scone, departs for his own region of Fife, a gesture of defiance:

Ross: Will you to Scone?
Macduff: No, cousin, I'll to Fife.
Ross: Well, I will thither.
Macduff: Well may you see things well done there. Adieu,
Lest our old robes sit easier than our new.
Ross: Farewell, father.
Old Man: God's benison go with you, and with those
That would make good of bad, and friends of foes.

act 2, scene 4, lines 35–41

The Old Man's benison or blessing can be read as a reproof of Ross, yet seems wistful. Masterfully, Shakespeare ends the scene of murder on a diminished note.

CHAPTER 5

Tear to Pieces
That Great Bond /
Which Keeps Me Pale

Banquo enters with a remarkable monologue marked by acute ambivalence:

> Thou hast it now, King, Cawdor, Glamis, all,
> As the weïrd women promised, and I fear
> Thou played'st most foully for't. Yet it was said
> It should not stand in thy posterity,
> But that myself should be the root and father
> Of many kings. If there come truth from them,
> As upon thee, Macbeth, their speeches shine,
> Why, by the verities on thee made good,
> May they not be my oracles as well,
> And set me up in hope? But hush, no more.
>
> act 3, scene 1, lines 1–10

Clearly Banquo suspects that Macbeth is the murderer, but he rightly apprehends that he, not Macbeth, will father a line of kings, stretching from his son Fleance down to King James I. You can argue that he becomes complicit in Macbeth's guilt, but I find that dubious. There is little he can do against Macbeth, who is quick, after Banquo departs, to cut him down:

> To be thus is nothing, but to be safely thus:
> Our fears in Banquo stick deep,
> And in his royalty of nature reigns that
> Which would be feared.

Macbeth's soliloquies are ruthlessly economical. His kingship is equivocal unless it can be secured. His anxieties concerning Banquo are deeply inward, yet they become a dagger that will stick or thrust into Banquo and so end him.

>   'Tis much he dares,
> And to that dauntless temper of his mind,
> He hath a wisdom that doth guide his valour
> To act in safety.

The contrast with Macbeth may not be intended, and yet both captains share the ability to master their fears. It is Macbeth who lacks the wisdom to guide his own courage to safe harbor.

>   There is none but he,
> Whose being I do fear; and under him
> My genius is rebuked, as it is said
> Mark Antony's was by Caesar.

MACBETH: A DAGGER OF THE MIND

Banquo is unique since his continued existence frightens Macbeth. Just as the soothsayer in *Antony and Cleopatra* warns Antony to keep his distance from Octavius, because the younger man diminishes Antony's guardian spirit, so Macbeth's tutelary genius wanes in Banquo's presence.

> He chid the sisters
> When first they put the name of king upon me,
> And bade them speak to him. Then, prophet-like,
> They hailed him father to a line of kings.
> Upon my head they placed a fruitless crown
> And put a barren sceptre in my gripe,
> Thence to be wrenched with an unlineal hand,
> No son of mine succeeding.

To hold the sceptre in your gripe or grasp is barren, when Banquo's descendants will be king.

> If 't be so,
> For Banquo's issue have I filed my mind;
> For them, the gracious Duncan have I murdered;
> Put rancours in the vessel of my peace
> Only for them; and mine eternal jewel
> Given to the common enemy of man,
> To make them kings, the seeds of Banquo kings.
> Rather than so, come fate into the list,
> And champion me to th'utterance. Who's there?

act 3, scene 1, lines 47–71

There is extraordinary bitterness in Macbeth's sense of defilement, if all his guilt has brought him is to have made kings of Banquo's descendants. "The vessel of my peace" is the poisoned communion chalice, and Macbeth's eternal jewel or soul has been given to Satan, "the common enemy of man." In a strong metaphor, Macbeth calls for fate to come into the place of tournaments, and to "champion" or fight for him "to th'utterance," that is to say, to the death.

Two hired murderers enter, to be coached by Macbeth:

Macbeth: Was it not yesterday we spoke together?
Murderers: It was, so please your highness.
Macbeth: Well then,
Now have you considered of my speeches?
Know, that it was he, in the times past,
Which held you so under fortune,
Which you thought had been our innocent self.
This I made good to you, in our last conference,
Passed in probation with you:
How you were borne in hand, how crossed;
The instruments, who wrought with them,
And all things else, that might
To half a soul, and to a notion crazed,
Say, 'Thus did Banquo.'
1 Murderer: You made it known to us.
Macbeth: I did so; and went further, which is now
Our point of second meeting. Do you find
Your patience so predominant in your nature

MACBETH: A DAGGER OF THE MIND

That you can let this go? Are you so gospelled
To pray for this good man, and for his issue,
Whose heavy hand hath bowed you to the grave,
And beggared yours forever?

We are not told what the past relation of these killers was to Banquo. Evidently he judged soundly that these ruffians merited virtually nothing. There is a bitter savagery, new to Macbeth, in his sarcastic question as to whether they are so Christian as to pray for Banquo and Fleance. Fiercely cataloguing them as dogs, he rouses their self-contempt to the work of slaughter:

1 Murderer: We are men, my liege.
Macbeth: Ay, in the catalogue ye go for men:
As hounds and greyhounds, mongrels, spaniels, curs,
Shoughs, water-rugs and demi-wolves are clept
All by the name of dogs. The valued file
Distinguishes the swift, the slow, the subtle,
The housekeeper, the hunter, every one
According to the gift which bounteous nature
Hath in him closed, whereby he does receive
Particular addition, from the bill
That writes them all alike: and so of men.
Now, if you have a station in the file
Not i'th' worst rank of manhood, say't,
And I will put that business in your bosoms,
Whose execution takes your enemy off,
Grapples you to the heart and love of us,

Who wear our health but sickly in his life,

Which in his death were perfect.

2 Murderer: I am one, my liege

Whom the vile blows and buffets of the world

Hath so incensed, that I am reckless what

I do to spite the world.

1 Murderer: And I another

So weary with disasters, tugged with fortune,

That I would set my life on any chance,

To mend it, or be rid on't.

Macbeth: Both of you know Banquo was your enemy.

Murderers: True, my lord.

Macbeth: So is he mine; and in such bloody distance

That every minute of his being thrusts

Against my near'st of life: and though I could

With bare-faced power sweep him from my sight

And bid my will avouch it, yet I must not,

For certain friends that are both his and mine,

Whose loves I may not drop, but wail his fall

Who I myself struck down. And thence it is,

That I to your assistance do make love,

Masking the business from the common eye

For sundry weighty reasons.

2 Murderer: We shall, my lord,

Perform what you command us.

1 Murderer: Though our lives—

Macbeth: Your spirits shine through you. Within this hour at most,

I will advise you where to plant yourselves,
Acquaint you with the perfect spy o'th' time,
The moment on't—for't must be done tonight,
And something from the palace:

"The perfect spy o'th' time" is ambiguous, but seems to mean keeping appropriate watch.

                        always thought
That I require a clearness—and with him,
To leave no rubs nor botches in the work,
Fleance, his son, that keeps him company,
Whose absence is no less material to me
Than is his father's, must embrace the fate
Of that dark hour. Resolve yourselves apart;
I'll come to you anon.
Murderers: We are resolved, my lord.
Macbeth: I'll call upon you straight: abide within.

                        [Exeunt Murderers.]
It is concluded: Banquo, thy soul's flight
If it find heaven, must find it out tonight.

                    act 3, scene 1, lines 73–144

That chilling couplet intensifies a new Macbeth. As he overhears himself, he changes more and more into the author of a tragedy of blood. His imagination itself has become bloody. He seems to move in an augmenting phantasmagoria of blood. Everything that he fears opposes him becomes so much blood. You can name it nature in the sense that Macbeth opposes nature. This answering force makes him a dagger, thrusting to shed more blood. "It will have blood, they say: blood will have blood."

Lady Macbeth also changes. As he becomes fiercer, she subsides. Their mutual passion ebbs as the stress of their condition magnifies:

> **Lady Macbeth:** Is Banquo gone from court?
> **Gentleman:** Ay, madam, but returns again tonight.
> **Lady Macbeth:** Say to the King I would attend his leisure
> For a few words.
>
> act 3, scene 2, lines 1–4

The fraying of their love is marked by a surging alienation. Lady Macbeth's ceremonial language jars when we recall the floodtide of their eros. Something frustrate and desperate enters her tone.

> **Gentleman:**   Madam, I will.   *Exit.*
> **Lady Macbeth:** Naught's had, all's spent,
> Where our desire is got without content.
> 'Tis safer to be that which we destroy,
> Than by destruction dwell in doubtful joy.
>
> act 3, scene 2, lines 4–8

She has it now and sees she has nothing. Desire has been squandered, and there is a dark envy of the slain Duncan, safe in his tomb, while she lives on in an uncertain pleasure of power.

Enter Macbeth.

Lady Macbeth: How now, my lord, why do you keep alone?
Of sorriest fancies your companions making,
Using those thoughts which should indeed have died
With them they think on? Things without all remedy
Should be without regard: what's done, is done.

act 3, scene 2, lines 9–13

It is a weak chiding because her anguish exceeds his.

Macbeth: We have scorched the snake, not killed it:
She'll close, and be herself, whilst our poor malice
Remains in danger of her former tooth.
But let the frame of things disjoint, both the worlds suffer,
Ere we will eat our meal in fear, and sleep
In the affliction of these terrible dreams
That shake us nightly. Better be with the dead,
Whom we, to gain our peace, have sent to peace,
Than on the torture of the mind to lie
In restless ecstasy. Duncan is in his grave.
After life's fitful fever, he sleeps well;
Treason has done his worst: nor steel, nor poison,
Malice domestic, foreign levy, nothing,
Can touch him further.

act 3, scene 2, lines 14–27

They have scored the snake, slashing with a dagger, but the serpent joins up and recovers her former strength. Macbeth, accusing

himself of poor malice or inadequate slaughter, rouses himself to an apocalyptic ambition to tear apart the universe itself, destroying this world and the world to come. Life itself is but a fitful fever.

Lady Macbeth: Come on. Gentle my lord,
Sleek o'er your rugged looks, be bright and jovial
Among your guests tonight.
Macbeth: So shall I, love, and so I pray be you.
Let your remembrance apply to Banquo,
Present him eminence, both with eye and tongue.
Unsafe the while, that we must lave
Our honours in these flattering streams,
And make our faces vizards to our hearts,
Disguising what they are.

                              act 3, scene 2, lines 27–36

There is a profound puzzle in this. He knows Banquo will not be there and yet he dwells on the edge of the night world. In a dark irony, he has an intimation of Banquo's ghost coming to the feast.

Lady Macbeth: You must leave this.
Macbeth: O, full of scorpions is my mind, dear wife:
Thou know'st that Banquo and his Fleance lives.
Lady Macbeth: But in them nature's copy's not eterne.
Macbeth: There's comfort yet: they are assailable.
Then be thou jocund; ere the bat hath flown
His cloistered flight, ere to black Hecate's summons

The shard-borne beetle with his drowsy hums,
Hath rung night's yawning peal, there shall be done
A deed of dreadful note.

act 3, scene 2, lines 36–45

Macbeth is so far in fury that scorpions index his mind. "Comfort" and "jocund" become affects of poison. Poet of night, King Macbeth has a vision of the black bat rising up from cloistered ruins, before black Hecate, goddess of witches, calls up the humming beetle from its shard or dung. "Night's yawning peal" is both bell-ringing and the primal abyss, from which a false creation emanates.

Lady Macbeth: What's to be done?
Macbeth: Be innocent of the knowledge, dearest chuck,
Till thou applaud the deed. Come, seeling night,
Scarf up the tender eye of pitiful day
And with thy bloody and invisible hand
Cancel and tear to pieces that great bond
Which keeps me pale.

act 3, scene 2, lines 45–51

Macbeth's language surpasses itself in these invocations. The night is "seeling," in the sense of blinding a falcon while training him. The tender eye or sun of the pitiful day is scarfed up and so blindfolded. The night itself is an invisible hand and bloody dagger, urged to end and rip up that great bond of mankind, which keeps the usurper king within limits.

59

Macbeth: Light thickens
And the crow makes wing to th' rooky wood.
Good things of day begin to droop and drowse,
Whiles night's black agents to their preys do rouse.
Thou marvell'st at my words: but hold thee still;
Things bad begun, make strong themselves by ill.
So prithee, go with me.

                                        act 3, scene 2, lines 51–57

The large black crows, devourers of carrion, fly forth and complete the scene. And Macbeth also is completed and moves toward his private apocalypse.

CHAPTER 6

We Are Yet
but Young in Deed

The assassination of Banquo commences with the mystery of the third Murderer:

Enter three Murderers.
1 Murderer: But who did bid thee join with us?
3 Murderer: Macbeth.
2 Murderer: He needs not our mistrust, since he delivers
Our offices, and what we have to do,
To the direction just.

The third Murderer is laconic, starting with the simple "Macbeth." The other murderers realize they need not mistrust the mysterious third, since he knows their duties as to the ironically named just direction. As a despot, Macbeth trusts no one except his wife, and sends the third Murderer to spy upon the others.

1 Murderer: Then stand with us.
The west yet glimmers with some streaks of day.
Now spurs the lated traveller apace

To gain the timely inn, and near approaches
The subject of our watch.
3 Murderer: Hark, I hear horses.

In the twilight, the third Murderer is the first to hear the approach of Banquo and Fleance.

Banquo: [*within*] Give us a light there, ho!
2 Murderer: Then 'tis he: the rest,
That are within the note of expectation,
Already are i'th' court.
1 Murderer: His horses go about.

The horses are being led to the castle by grooms, while Banquo and Fleance walk a good distance to the royal castle.

3 Murderer: Almost a mile; but he does usually,
So all men do, from hence to the palace gate
Make it their walk.

The third Murderer is the best informed, and presumably is one of Macbeth's soldiers, possibly Seyton.

Enter Banquo and Fleance, with a torch.
2 Murderer: A light, a light.
3 Murderer: 'Tis he.

MACBETH: A DAGGER OF THE MIND

As might be expected, it is the third Murderer who verifies Banquo's identity.

1 Murderer: Stand to't.
Banquo: It will be rain tonight.
1 Murderer: Let it come down.

I never get out of my head that abrupt "Let it come down." The vicious irony informs the rain of dagger thrusts at the unarmed Banquo.

Banquo: O treachery!
[*The Murderers attack. First Murderer strikes out the light.*]
Fly, good Fleance, fly, fly, fly.
Thou mayst revenge—   [*Exit Fleance.*]
O slave!   [*Dies.*]

The revenge of Fleance is to establish a line of Scottish kings.

3 Murderer: Who did strike out the light?
1 Murderer: Was't not the way?
3 Murderer: There's but one down: the son is fled.

Again taking charge, the third Murderer angrily asks who has stifled the torch, allowing Fleance to escape in darkness, and grimly mutters, "There's but one down."

2 Murderer: We have lost
Best half of our affair.
1 Murderer: Well, let's away,
And say how much is done.

act 3, scene 3, lines 1–21

In what other play by Shakespeare could this spasm of a scene convey so strongly the essence of the protagonist, who is himself not present? The furtive intensity of this murder reverberates throughout the rest of *Macbeth*.

The escape of Fleance is the onset of the fall of Macbeth. His increasingly desperate efforts to control his own destiny, with the equivocal aid of the Weird Sisters, will be thwarted by his own augmenting violence. The downward turn is evident in the banquet scene, immediately following the murder of Banquo. Lady Macbeth presides while the anxious King seats himself among the thanes, urging his nervous subjects to be merry and drink copiously of the red wine. Abruptly wine changes to blood, as Macbeth goes to the door to receive the first Murderer's report:

Macbeth: See, they encounter thee with their hearts' thanks.
Both sides are even: here I'll sit i'th' midst.
Be large in mirth; anon we'll drink a measure
The table round.—There's blood upon thy face.
1 Murderer: 'Tis Banquo's then.
Macbeth: 'Tis better thee without than
    he within.

act 3, scene 4, lines 8–12

This peculiar jest itself indicates Macbeth's hardening nature, as does all his subsequent play of language.

Macbeth: Is he dispatched?
1 Murderer: My lord, his throat is cut; that I did for him.
Macbeth: Thou art the best o'th' cut-throats;
Yet he's good that did the like for Fleance.
If thou didst it, thou art the nonpareil.
1 Murderer: Most royal sir, Fleance is scaped.
Macbeth: Then comes my fit again: I had else been perfect;
Whole as the marble, founded as the rock,
As broad and general as the casing air:
But now I am cabined, cribbed, confined, bound in
To saucy doubts and fears. But Banquo's safe?

act 3, scene 4, lines 13–23

The revelation comes to Macbeth as a seizure. His vision of his own perfection or completion is beyond the human. He would be hard as marble or rock, securely based and as free as the enclosing air. Instead he is shut up in the cabin of himself, cribbed like an animal in a stall, imprisoned by insolent doubts and fears.

1 Murderer: Ay, my good lord: safe in a ditch he bides,
With twenty trenched gashes on his head,
The least a death to nature.
Macbeth: Thanks for that.
There the grown serpent lies; the worm that's fled
Hath nature that in time will venom breed,

No teeth for th' present. Get thee gone, tomorrow
We'll hear ourselves again.   [*Exit First Murderer.*]

act 3, scene 4, lines 24–30

The snake Banquo is scotched. Fleance, a mere worm, will be dangerous only in the future. The Murderer is dismissed, and Macbeth returns to his guests, and to the ghost of Banquo:

Lady Macbeth: My royal lord,
You do not give the cheer: the feast is sold
That is not often vouched, while 'tis a-making,
'Tis given with welcome. To feed were best at home:
From thence, the sauce to meat is ceremony,
Meeting were bare without it.

act 3, scene 4, lines 30–35

The fearful thanes accept her forced hospitality. Her call for ceremony is answered directly by the spirit of Banquo:

Enter the Ghost of Banquo, and sits in Macbeth's place.
Macbeth: Sweet remembrancer.
Now good digestion wait on appetite,
And health on both.

The "remembrancer" is ironic; indeed Lady Macbeth reminds him, but a remembrancer was a debt collector.

Lennox: May't please your Highness sit.

Macbeth: Here had we now our country's honour roof'd,

Were the grac'd person of our Banquo present,

Who may I rather challenge for unkindness

Than pity for mischance.

Ross: His absence, sir,

Lays blame upon his promise. Please't your highness

To grace us with your royal company?

Macbeth: The table's full.

Lennox: Here is a place reserved, sir.

Macbeth: Where?

Lennox: Here my good lord. What is't that moves your

     highness?

Macbeth: Which of you have done this?

Lords: What, my good lord?

Macbeth: Thou canst not say I did it: never shake

Thy gory locks at me.

                         act 3, scene 4, lines 35–48

Only Macbeth can see the ghost. Banquo now usurps the usurper's place.

Ross: Gentlemen, rise; his highness is not well.

Lady Macbeth: Sit, worthy friends; my lord is often thus,

And hath been from his youth. Pray you keep seat,

The fit is momentary; upon a thought

He will again be well. If much you note him
You shall offend him, and extend his passion.
Feed, and regard him not. [*to Macbeth*] Are you a man?
Macbeth: Ay, and a bold one, that dare look on that
Which might appal the devil.
Lady Macbeth: O, proper stuff.
This is the very painting of your fear:
This is the air-drawn dagger which you said
Led you to Duncan. O, these flaws and starts,
Impostors to true fear, would well become
A woman's story at a winter's fire,
Authorized by her grandam. Shame itself.
Why do you make such faces? When all's done
You look but on a stool.

The dagger of the mind has returned.

Macbeth: Prithee see there.
Behold, look, lo, how say you?
[*to Ghost*] Why, what care I? If thou canst nod, speak too.
act 3, scene 4, lines 49–67

Unique among Shakespeare's ghosts, the spirit of Banquo is voiceless, but its nod is eloquent.

Macbeth: If charnel-houses and our graves must send
Those that we bury back, our monuments

Shall be the maws of kites.   [*Exit Ghost.*]

Lady Macbeth: What? Quite unmanned in folly.

Macbeth: If I stand here, I saw him.

Lady Macbeth: Fie, for shame.

Macbeth: Blood hath been shed ere now, i'th' olden time,

Ere humane statute purged the gentle weal;

Ay, and since too, murders have been performed

Too terrible for the ear. The times have been,

That when the brains were out, the man would die,

And there an end. But now they rise again

With twenty mortal murders on their crowns,

And push us from our stools. This is more strange

Than such a murder is.

act 3, scene 4, lines 68–81

Macbeth's incessant, preternatural rhetoric of power achieves another summit here. "Humane" for Shakespeare need not mean compassionate, but only "human" or made by man. When I lie abed sleeplessly at night, and think of *Macbeth*, frequently I hear:

> The time has been,
> That when the brains were out, the man would die,
> And there an end;

The tone is one of outrage, and will dominate Macbeth's utterances until the end of the play. He laments the olden time, when murder possessed finality. Banquo rises from the dead and pushes Macbeth from his throne. There is a lingering, dying fall in:

> This is more strange
> Than such a murder is.

Strangeness becomes the garment of outrage. When I was in my thirties and he was in his sixties, I lunched several times with the late critic Owen Barfield in London. We stayed in touch after that and I corresponded with him when I edited an anthology, *Romanticism and Consciousness* (1970), and included, by his advice, the remarkable chapter "Symptoms of Iconoclasm" from his *Saving the Appearances: A Study in Idolatry* (1957). Though that book and his immensely useful *History in English Words* (1926) continue to influence me, I owe even more to his *Poetic Diction: A Study in Meaning* (1928). Its eleventh chapter, "Strangeness," completed for me the critical reveries on strangeness by the Aesthetic Critic proper, Walter Pater.

"It must be a strangeness of *meaning*," Barfield remarked, and elaborated magnificently:

> It is not correlative with wonder; for wonder is our reaction to things which we are conscious of not quite understanding, or at any rate of understanding less than we had thought. The element of strangeness in beauty has the contrary effect. It arises from contact with a different kind of *consciousness* from our own, different, yet not so remote that we cannot partly share it, as indeed, in such a connection, the mere word "contact" implies.

Strangeness, in fact, arouses wonder when we do not understand; aesthetic imagination when we do.

Macbeth's imagination increasingly assumes the garment of
strangeness, and fuses our sense of wonder at what we barely understand. We identify with his outrage as his stratagems fall short of
the security he longs to possess. The aesthetics of outrage are a
branch of the strangeness of meaning. It is very difficult not to sympathize with a powerful representation of outrage, whether comic
or tragic. Death is the ultimate outrage, and the murderous Macbeth becomes baffled when blood fails him.

Summoned back to the feast by Lady Macbeth, the usurper
King is again overcome by the apparition of Banquo:

Lady Macbeth: My worthy lord,
Your noble friends do lack you.
Macbeth: I do forget.
Do not muse at me, my most worthy friends,
I have a strange infirmity, which is nothing
To those that know me. Come, love and health to all,
Then I'll sit down. Give me some wine, fill full.
Enter Ghost.
I drink to the general joy o'the whole table,
And to our dear friend Banquo, whom we miss—
Would he were here. To all, and him we thirst,
And all to all.

act 3, scene 4, lines 81–90

71

The savage irony of saying would that Banquo were here is enhanced by "and him we thirst," since thirst means "long for."

Lords: Our duties, and the pledge.
Macbeth: Avaunt, and quit my sight! Let the earth hide thee.
Thy bones are marrowless, thy blood is cold;
Thou hast no speculation in those eyes
Which thou dost glare with.

act 3, scene 4, lines 90–94

To be marrowless is to lack all substance, and the rich word "speculation" implies an intelligence of seeing, as opposed to the fixed look of "glare."

Lady Macbeth: Think of this, good peers,
But as a thing of custom; 'tis no other,
Only it spoils the pleasure of the time.
Macbeth: What man dare, I dare.
Approach thou like the rugged Russian bear,
The armed rhinoceros, or the Hyrcan tiger,
Take any shape but that, and my firm nerves
Shall never tremble. Or be alive again,
And dare me to the desert with thy sword.

The fierce strength of the Russian bear, the rhinoceros with its horn, the Hyrcan tiger of Eastern Europe, would not daunt Macbeth. Or if Banquo were to resurrect and challenge his murderer to a death duel in some deserted place, Macbeth would greet this gladly.

Macbeth: If trembling I inhabit then, protest me
The baby of a girl. Hence, horrible shadow,
Unreal mockery, hence.   [*Exit Ghost.*]

The self-contempt of the great killer would proclaim itself as a little girl's doll. The Ghost departs and Macbeth is again a man.

Macbeth: Why so, being gone
I am a man again. [*to Lords*] Pray you, sit still.
                              act 3, scene 4, lines 94–106

By now the terrified thanes and their hostess have no desire to sit still:

Lady Macbeth: You have displaced the mirth, broke the good
        meeting
With most admired disorder.

"Admired" conveys astonishment.

Macbeth: Can such things be,
And overcome us like a summer's cloud,
Without our special wonder? You make me strange
Even to the disposition that I owe,
When now I think you can behold such sights
And keep the natural ruby of your cheeks
When mine is blanched with fear.
                              act 3, scene 4, lines 107–14

Strangeness is again the keynote. Overcome or surprised as by a cloud in summer, Macbeth is moved to woe and wonder. Estranged from his disposition or true nature, he forgets that only he has seen the Ghost.

Ross: What sights, my lord?
Lady Macbeth: I pray you speak not; he grows worse and
    worse;
Question enrages him. At once, goodnight.
Stand not upon the order of your going
But go at once.

Lady Macbeth utters what has become the classic dismissal of lingering guests. Rank can be forgotten; the thanes are expelled.

Lennox: Goodnight, and better health
Attend his majesty.
Lady Macbeth: A kind good night to all.   [*Exeunt Lords.*]
Macbeth: It will have blood they say: blood will have blood:
Stones have been known to move, and trees to speak;
Augures, and understood relations, have
By maggot-pies and choughs and rooks brought forth
The secret'st man of blood. What is the night?
Lady Macbeth: Almost at odds with morning, which is which.
                                        act 3, scene 4, lines 114–25

The echo of Genesis 9:6 is telling:

Who so sheddeth man's blood, by man shall his blood be shed:
  for in the image of God hath he made man.

Geneva Bible

In that spirit stones move and trees speak of murder. Auguries and unlikely relations have exposed even the most prudentially hidden murderer, in response to the sacrifices of magpies, crows, and rooks, proper use for such birds of ill omen.

Macbeth: How sayst thou that Macduff denies his person
At our great bidding?

Ominously, Macbeth asks his Queen to interpret Macduff's absence, despite a royal summons.

Lady Macbeth: Did you send to him, sir?
Macbeth: I hear it by the way; but I will send.
There's not a one of them but in his house
I keep a servant fee'd.

There is a paid informer in the home of every thane.

                I will tomorrow,
And betimes I will, to the weïrd sisters.
More shall they speak: for now I am bent to know
By the worst means, the worst;

Macbeth at the next dawn will brave the three Witches, determined to know the worst he has to fear.

---

                                    for mine own good,
All causes shall give way. I am in blood
Stepped in so far, that should I wade no more,
Returning were as tedious as go o'er.
Strange things I have in head, that will to hand,
Which must be acted, ere they may be scanned.

                              act 3, scene 4, lines 126–38

Scanning or close examination can wait upon action. "Strange things" are now the impending massacre of Lady Macduff and her little children.

Lady Macbeth: You lack the season of all natures, sleep.
Macbeth: Come, we'll to sleep. My strange and self-abuse
Is the initiate fear, that wants hard use.
We are yet but young in deed.

                              act 3, scene 4, lines 139–42

"My strange and self-abuse" again invokes strangeness, which for Macbeth means fresh outrages. He deprecates his "initiate fear" as the affect of a mere novice. His fearsome judgment is that it wants or lacks hard or pitiless use. We end upon a shudder of worse to come: "We are yet but young in deed."

What,
Will the Line Stretch Out
to th' Crack of Doom

The subsequent scene of the Witches and Hecate seems to me Shakespeare's, though there is an ongoing argument that assigns its composition to Thomas Middleton. Either way, it is rather less impressive than the earlier and later manifestations of the Weird Sisters. Hecate is rather petulant as she scolds the Witches:

Thunder. Enter the three Witches, meeting Hecate.
1 Witch: Why how now, Hecate? You look angerly.
Hecate: Have I not reason, beldams as you are,
Saucy and over-bold? How did you dare
To trade and traffic with Macbeth
In riddles and affairs of death;
And I, the mistress of your charms,
The close contriver of all harms,
Was never called to bear my part
Or show the glory of our art?

Hecate characterizes the witches as hags and scolds them as amateurs, compared to her glorious professionalism.

> And, which is worse, all you have done
> Hath been but for a wayward son,
> Spiteful and wrathful, who, as others do,
> Loves for his own ends, not for you.

To call Macbeth wayward or perverse, following only his own will, seems relevant enough to me.

> But make amends now; get you gone,
> And at the pit of Acheron
> Meet me i'th' morning; thither he
> Will come, to know his destiny.
> Your vessels and your spells provide,
> Your charms, and every thing beside.

She summons them to meet her in hell, where Acheron runs as one of seven rivers. They are to bring their vessels or utensils, and all that is necessary for their dark art:

> I am for th'air: this night I'll spend
> Unto a dismal and a fatal end.

Hecate is goddess of witchcraft, the night, and the moon. Evidently she is capable of flying, and intends to devote this particular night to malignity.

Great business must be wrought ere noon.
Upon the corner of the moon
There hangs a vaporous drop profound,
I'll catch it ere it come to ground;
And that, distilled by magic sleights,
Shall raise such artificial sprites
As by the strength of their illusion
Shall draw him on to his confusion.

The "vaporous drop" is a foam emanating from the moon that transfigures herbs into spells. Hecate will seize it before it touches earth and refine it by her magic tricks. She will raise up cunning spirits and employ their hallucinatory power to entrap Macbeth into a false security:

He shall spurn fate, scorn death, and bear
His hopes 'bove wisdom, grace and fear;
And you all know, security
Is mortals' chiefest enemy   *Music, and a song*
Hark, I am called: my little spirit, see,
Sits in a foggy cloud, and stays for me.   [*Exit.*]
[*Sing within.*] 'Come away, come away, *etc.*'
1 Witch: Come, let's make haste, she'll soon be back again.

act 3, scene 5, lines 1–36

A strangely ambiguous scene follows, in which Lennox and another lord exchange ironic observations on the murderous tyranny of Macbeth:

79

Lennox: My former speeches have but hit your thoughts
Which can interpret farther. Only I say
Things have been strangely borne. The gracious Duncan
Was pitied of Macbeth; marry, he was dead.
And the right-valiant Banquo walked too late,
Whom you may say, if 't please you, Fleance killed,
For Fleance fled: men must not walk too late.

Lennox remarks on his prior agreement with the other thane. "Strangely borne" or conducted returns the audience to the word "strange," which is used twenty times in this short play. This is one of the two "strangely"s, and becomes a synonym for mayhem. Indirectly, Lennox accuses Macbeth of both assassinations, Duncan's and Banquo's.

Who cannot want the thought how monstrous
It was for Malcolm and for Donalbain
To kill their gracious father? Damned fact,
How it did grieve Macbeth! Did he not straight,
In pious rage, the two delinquents tear,
That were the slaves of drink and thralls of sleep?
Was not that nobly done? Ay, and wisely too:
For 'twould have angered any heart alive
To hear the men deny't. So that I say,
He has borne all things well, and I do think
That had he Duncan's sons under his key,
As, an't please heaven, he shall not, they should find

What 'twere to kill a father; so should Fleance.

act 3, scene 6, lines 1–20

"Want the thought" means just the reverse of what it says. Lennox is sardonic as he praises the "pious rage" of Macbeth, and his wisdom in butchering the drunken grooms. "Strangely borne" now becomes "borne all things well" and intimates revulsion. Malcolm, Donalbain, and Fleance have saved themselves by flight, and Lennox at last gives up the irony with "an't please heaven, he shall not."

But peace; for from broad words, and 'cause he failed
His presence at the tyrant's feast, I hear
Macduff lives in disgrace. Sir, can you tell
Where he bestows himself?

Macduff's broad or honest words, and his absence from the Macbeths' banquet, have placed him in danger.

Lord: The son of Duncan,
From whom this tyrant holds the due of birth,
Lives in the English court, and is received
Of the most pious Edward with such grace
That the malevolence of fortune nothing
Takes from his high respect. Thither Macduff
Is gone, to pray the holy king, upon his aid
To wake Northumberland, and warlike Siward,
That by the help of these, with Him above

To ratify the work, we may again
Give to our tables meat, sleep to our nights,
Free from our feasts and banquets bloody knives;
Do faithful homage and receive free honours,
All which we pine for now. And this report
Hath so exasperate their king, that he
Prepares for some attempt of war.

> act 3, scene 6, lines 21–39

Malcolm is the honored guest of the English King Edward the Confessor, and Siward, the Earl of Northumberland, will join Malcolm and Macduff in the battle against the furious Macbeth.

Lennox: Sent he to Macduff?
Lord: He did. And with an absolute, 'Sir, not I'
The cloudy messenger turns me his back
And hums, as who should say, 'You'll rue the time
That clogs me with this answer.'

Macduff's refusal—"Sir, not I"—sends away the scowling messenger and provokes Macbeth's own version of the massacre of the innocents.

Lennox: And that well might
Advise him to a caution, t'hold what distance
His wisdom can provide. Some holy angel
Fly to the court of England and unfold

His message ere he come, that a swift blessing
May soon return to this our suffering country,
Under a hand accursed.
Lord: I'll send my prayers with him.

act 3, scene 6, lines 40–50

With those prayers still resonating, Shakespeare gives us the extraordinary scene of Macbeth confronting the Weird Sisters:

Thunder. Enter the three Witches.
1 Witch: Thrice the brinded cat hath mewed.
2 Witch: Thrice, and once the hedge-pig whined.
3 Witch: Harpier cries, ''Tis time, 'tis time.'

The three familiars—tawny cat, hedgehog, and the oddly named Harpier—set the time for the fatal interview. Keep in mind that "time," in all its forms, is used fifty-two times in *Macbeth*.

1 Witch: Round about the cauldron go;
In the poisoned entrails throw.
Toad, that under cold stone
Days and nights has thirty-one
Sweltered venom sleeping got,
Boil thou first i'th' charmed pot.
All: Double, double, toil and trouble;
Fire burn, and cauldron bubble.
2 Witch: Fillet of a fenny snake,

In the cauldron boil and bake;
Eye of newt and toe of frog,
Wool of bat and tongue of dog,
Adder's fork and blind-worm's sting,
Lizard's leg and howlet's wing,
For a charm of powerful trouble,
Like a hell-broth boil and bubble.
All: Double, double, toil and trouble;
Fire burn, and cauldron bubble.
3 Witch: Scale of dragon, tooth of wolf,
Witch's mummy, maw and gulf
Of the ravined salt-sea shark,
Root of hemlock digged i'th' dark,
Liver of blaspheming Jew,
Gall of goat, and slips of yew
Slivered in the moon's eclipse,
Nose of Turk and Tartar's lips,
Finger of birth-strangled babe
Ditch-delivered by a drab,
Make the gruel thick and slab.
Add thereto a tiger's chawdron,
For th'ingredience of our cauldron.
All: Double, double, toil and trouble;
Fire burn, and cauldron bubble.
2 Witch: Cool it with a baboon's blood,
Then the charm is firm and good.

act 4, scene 1, lines 1–38

This is famously all good unclean fun, particularly my favorite line: "Liver of blaspheming Jew." It stages splendidly, and is a darksome frolic. To analyze it would be pedantic.

Enter Hecate and the other three Witches.

Hecate: O, well done. I commend your pains,

And every one shall share i'th' gains.

And now about the cauldron sing,

Like elves and fairies in a ring,

Enchanting all that you put in.

[*Music and a song:* 'Black spirits,' *etc.*]

[*Exeunt Hecate and the three other Witches.*]

2 Witch: By the pricking of my thumbs,

Something wicked this way comes.

act 4, scene 1, lines 39–45

That celebrated line—"Something wicked this way comes"—has an eminence transcending even the advent of Macbeth:

2 Witch: Open locks, whoever knocks.

Enter Macbeth.

Macbeth: How now, you secret, black and midnight hags?

What is't you do?

All: A deed without a name.

Macbeth: I conjure you, by that which you profess,

Howe'er you come to know it, answer me;

Though you untie the winds and let them fight

Against the churches, though the yeasty waves
Confound and swallow navigation up,
Though bladed corn be lodged and trees blown down,
Though castles topple on their warders' heads,
Though palaces and pyramids do slope
Their heads to their foundations, though the treasure
Of Nature's germen tumble altogether
Even till destruction sicken, answer me
To what I ask you.

act 4, scene 1, lines 46–60

In a mockery of invoking the sacred, Macbeth exhorts and also encourages the Witches to precipitate apocalypse. The five-fold "though" brushes aside the destruction of churches, ships, new corn, trees, castles, palaces, obelisks, even the storehouse of nature's germen, or seeds. With gusto, Macbeth speaks of destruction itself sickening, glutted by its own violence. All this is as nothing, compared to the tyrant's lust for security:

1 Witch: Speak.
2 Witch: Demand.
3 Witch: We'll answer.
1 Witch: Say, if thou'dst rather hear it from our mouths,
Or from our masters?

"Masters" here is a magician's term, and refers to the unseen powers that manipulate the Apparitions.

Macbeth: Call 'em, let me see 'em.

1 Witch: Pour in sow's blood that hath eaten

Her nine farrow; grease that's sweaten

From the murderer's gibbet, throw

Into the flame.

All: Come high or low,

Thy self and office deftly show. *Thunder.*

Enter First Apparition: an armed head.

Macbeth: Tell me, thou unknown power—

1 Witch: He knows thy thought:

Hear his speech, but say thou nought.

1 Apparition: Macbeth, Macbeth, Macbeth. Beware Macduff,

Beware the Thane of Fife. Dismiss me. Enough. *He descends.*

Macbeth: Whate'er thou art, for thy good caution, thanks;

Thou hast harped my fear aright. But one word more—

"Harped" might mean "surmised," and may be based on the plucking of a harp string.

1 Witch: He will not be commanded. Here's another,

More potent than the first. *Thunder.*

Enter Second Apparition: a bloody child.

2 Apparition: Macbeth. Macbeth. Macbeth.

Macbeth: Had I three ears, I'd hear thee.

2 Apparition: Be bloody, bold, and resolute: laugh to scorn

The power of man, for none of woman born

Shall harm Macbeth. *Descends.*

Macbeth: Then live, Macduff: what need I fear of thee?

But yet I'll make assurance double sure,

And take a bond of fate: thou shalt not live,

That I may tell pale-hearted fear it lies

And sleep in spite of thunder.   *Thunder.*

act 4, scene 1, lines 60–85

The augmenting blood-madness of Macbeth befits this drama, where "blood" or "bloody" occurs forty-one times, second only to "time" itself. He begins to believe that anyone alive must be killed, children in particular.

Enter Third Apparition: a child crowned, with a tree in his hand.

Macbeth: What is this,

That rises like the issue of a king

And wears upon his baby-brow the round

And top of sovereignty?

The crowned child descends from kings, and could be Malcolm or Fleance.

All: Listen, but speak not to't.

3 Apparition: Be lion-mettled, proud, and take no care

Who chafes, who frets, or where conspirers are.

Macbeth shall never vanquished be, until

Great Birnam Wood to high Dunsinane Hill

Shall come against him.   *Descends.*

Macbeth: That will never be.

88

Who can impress the forest, bid the tree
Unfix his earth-bound root? Sweet bodements, good.

The bodements are fortunate omens, but they are equivocal and Macbeth misinterprets them.

Macbeth: Rebellious dead, rise never till the Wood
Of Birnam rise, and our high-placed Macbeth
Shall live the lease of nature, pay his breath
To time and mortal custom. Yet my heart
Throbs to know one thing: tell me, if your art
Can tell so much, shall Banquo's issue ever
Reign in this kingdom?

What shall we make of Macbeth's strange speaking of himself in the third person? It may be that suddenly he sees himself with a new perspective. Is he merely yet one more king of Scotland, who will not even live out a normal life span?

All: Seek to know no more.
Macbeth: I will be satisfied. Deny me this,
And an eternal curse fall on you. Let me know.
Why sinks that cauldron, and what noise is this?   *Hautboys.*

act 4, scene 1, lines 85–105

Macbeth's fury of apprehension is unappeasable and turns to another anxiety of futurity. Has he not waded through blood fecklessly, since Banquo's descendants constitute the royal line of Scotland?

1 Witch: Show.

2 Witch: Show.

3 Witch: Show.

All: Show his eyes, and grieve his heart;

Come like shadows, so depart.

A show of eight kings, the last with a glass in his hand; and

     Banquo.

Macbeth: Thou art too like the spirit of Banquo; down:

Thy crown does sear mine eyeballs. And thy hair,

Thou other gold-bound brow, is like the first.

A third is like the former. Filthy hags,

Why do you show me this?—A fourth? Start, eyes!

What, will the line stretch out to th' crack of doom?

                          act 4, scene 1, lines 106–16

Sigmund Freud, who placed *Macbeth* first among Shakespeare's works, jovially quoted that last apocalyptic question, when he contemplated his own endless series of books. *Macbeth* seems to have been John Milton's favorite play, and I sometimes brood that Freud had a particular passion for Milton. Ambition unrestrained binds together Macbeth, Milton, and Freud.

Macbeth: Another yet? A seventh? I'll see no more;

And yet the eighth appears, who bears a glass

Which shows me many more; and some I see

That twofold balls and treble sceptres carry.

Horrible sight. Now I see 'tis true;

For the blood-boltered Banquo smiles upon me
And points at them for his.   [*Exeunt kings and Banquo.*]

act 4, scene 1, lines 117–23

The glass presumably is magical and is employed for divination. The twofold balls may signify the union of Scotland and England under James I, while the treble sceptres may refer to England, Scotland, and Wales. Triumphantly Banquo exults, though his hair is clotted with blood.

Macbeth: What? Is this so?
1 Witch: Ay, sir, all this is so. But why
Stands Macbeth thus amazedly?
Come, sisters, cheer we up his sprites,
And show the best of our delights.
I'll charm the air to give a sound,
While you perform your antic round,
That this great king may kindly say
Our duties did his welcome pay.

Music. The Witches dance and vanish.

act 4, scene 1, lines 123–31

It is gleefully grotesque that the Weird Sisters rejoice in their message, and seek to entertain the distracted King.

Macbeth: Where are they? Gone? Let this pernicious hour
Stand aye accursed in the calendar.

Come in, without there.

Enter Lennox.

Lennox: What's your Grace's will?

Macbeth: Saw you the weïrd sisters?

Lennox: No, my lord.

Macbeth: Came they not by you?

Lennox: No indeed, my lord.

Macbeth: Infected be the air whereon they ride,

And damned all those that trust them. I did hear

The galloping of horse. Who was't came by?

Lennox: 'Tis two or three, my lord, that bring you word

Macduff is fled to England.

Macbeth: Fled to England?

Lennox: Ay, my good lord.

Macbeth: Time, thou anticipat'st my dread exploits.

The flighty purpose never is o'ertook

Unless the deed go with it.

act 4, scene 1, lines 132–45

Time has forestalled Macbeth's murder of Macduff. Between purpose and accomplishment, the shadow of time intervenes, however swift the intention. Resolution now mounts in Macbeth to his greatest iniquity: the slaughter of Lady Macduff, her children, and his entire household.

From this moment

The very firstlings of my heart shall be

The firstlings of my hand. And even now,

To crown my thoughts with acts, be it thought and done.

The castle of Macduff I will surprise,

Seize upon Fife, give to th'edge o'th' sword

His wife, his babes, and all unfortunate souls

That trace him in his line. No boasting like a fool;

This deed I'll do before this purpose cool.

But no more sights. Where are these gentlemen?

Come bring me where they are.

act 4, scene 1, lines 145–55

"Firstlings" is a fearsome irony, since these initial impulses suggest children. The cry of "But no more sights" is a further kindling of Macbeth's bloody desperation.

CHAPTER 8

Yet Who Would Have Thought the Old Man to Have Had So Much Blood in Him?

In this drama of surpassing cruelties, the slaughter of Lady Macduff and her children has a unique dreadfulness. It is marked by a pathos unbearably poignant. Shakespeare's skill is so extraordinary, even for him, that we hear no false notes in this threnody:

Enter Macduff's Wife, her Son, and Ross.
Lady Macduff: What had he done, to make him fly the land?
Ross: You must have patience, madam.
Lady Macduff: He had none;
His flight was madness. When our actions do not,
Our fears do make us traitors.

act 4, scene 2, lines 1–4

We have to wonder why Macduff did not take his wife, children, and household with him when he fled to England. Has he forgotten Banquo's superb outcry and his strong response?

Banquo: In the great hand of God I stand, and thence

Against the undivulged pretence I fight

Of treasonous malice.

Macduff: And so do I.

                              act 2, scene 3, lines 131–33

Ross: You know not

Whether it was his wisdom or his fear.

Lady Macduff: Wisdom? To leave his wife, to leave his babes,

His mansion and his titles in a place

From whence himself does fly? He loves us not;

He wants the natural touch. For the poor wren,

The most diminutive of birds, will fight,

Her young ones in her nest, against the owl.

All is the fear and nothing is the love;

As little is the wisdom, where the flight

So runs against all reason.

Lady Macduff is wonderfully spirited, particularly when she says of her husband: "He wants the natural touch."

Ross: My dearest coz,

I pray you school yourself. But for your husband,

He is noble, wise, judicious, and best knows

The fits o'th' season. I dare not speak much further;

But cruel are the times when we are traitors

And do not know ourselves; when we hold rumour

From what we fear, yet know not what we fear,

But float upon a wild and violent sea

Each way and move. I take my leave of you;

Shall not be long but I'll be here again.

Things at the worst will cease, or else climb upward

To what they were before. My pretty cousin,

Blessing upon you.

Lady Macduff: Fathered he is, and yet he's fatherless.

Ross: I am so much a fool, should I stay longer,

It would be my disgrace and your discomfort.

I take my leave at once.   [*Exit Ross.*]

act 4, scene 2, lines 4–30

You would think that Ross would stay to defend the threatened family, but like Lennox he is one more unstable thane. When he says to the little boy:

My pretty cousin,

Blessing upon you.

is that sufficient when he should make a stand to protect the child?

Lady Macduff: Sirrah, your father's dead. And what will you
    do now? How will you live?

Son: As birds do, mother.

Lady Macduff: What, with worms and flies?

Son: With what I get, I mean; and so do they.

Lady Macduff: Poor bird, thou'dst never fear the net nor lime,
The pitfall nor the gin.
Son: Why should I, mother? Poor birds they are not set for.
My father is not dead, for all your saying.

The spirited little boy is equal to his mother's steadfastness. We are captured by both of them, which makes the impending desolation yet more unbearable.

Lady Macduff: Yes, he is dead. How wilt thou do for a father?
Son: Nay, how will you do for a husband?
Lady Macduff: Why, I can buy me twenty at any market.
Son: Then you'll buy 'em to sell again.
Lady Macduff: Thou speak'st with all thy wit, and yet, i'faith,
With wit enough for thee.

Again we come to love them. In the face of death they charm us with their verve and wit.

Son: Was my father a traitor, mother?
Lady Macduff: Ay, that he was.
Son: What is a traitor?
Lady Macduff: Why, one that swears and lies.
Son: And be all traitors that do so?
Lady Macduff: Every one that does so is a traitor, and must be
hanged.
Son: And must they all be hanged that swear and lie?
Lady Macduff: Every one.

Son: Who must hang them?

Lady Macduff: Why, the honest men.

Son: Then the liars and swearers are fools, for there are liars
and swearers enow to beat the honest men, and hang up
them.

Reading and teaching this, I experience something like the exquisite torment inflicted upon Othello by Iago.

Lady Macduff: Now, God help thee, poor monkey. But how
wilt thou do for a father?

Son: If he were dead, you'd weep for him; if you would not, it
were a good sign that I should quickly have a new father.

Lady Macduff: Poor prattler, how thou talk'st.

act 4, scene 2, lines 31–65

I am torn between admiring Shakespeare's everliving art and wincing at its effect on me.

Enter a Messenger.

Messenger: Bless you, fair dame. I am not to you known,
Though in your state of honour I am perfect.
I doubt some danger does approach you nearly.
If you will take a homely man's advice,
Be not found here; hence with your little ones.
To fright you thus, methinks I am too savage;
To do worse to you were fell cruelty,
Which is too nigh your person. Heaven preserve you.

I dare abide no longer.   [*Exit Messenger.*]
Lady Macduff: Whither should I fly?
I have done no harm. But I remember now
I am in this earthly world, where to do harm
Is often laudable, to do good sometime
Accounted dangerous folly. Why then, alas,
Do I put up that womanly defence,
To say I have done no harm?

                                    act 4, scene 2, lines 66–81

The pathos goes beyond all limits. We realize again how marvelous a woman is about to be martyred.

Enter Murderers.
Lady Macduff: What are these faces?
1 Murderer: Where is your husband?
Lady Macduff: I hope, in no place so unsanctified
Where such as thou mayst find him.
1 Murderer: He's a traitor.
Son: Thou liest, thou shag-haired villain.
1 Murderer: What, you egg!
Young fry of treachery!
Son: He has killed me, mother.
Run away, I pray you.

                    [*Exit Lady Macduff crying* 'Murder.']
                            [*Exeunt Murderers.*]
                        act 4, scene 2, lines 81–87

100

This terrible enormity transcends commentary. Some critics condemn the next scene, where Malcolm and Macduff, in the proximity of the court of King Edward the Confessor, have a rather long and complex exchange:

Malcolm: Let us seek out some desolate shade and there
Weep our sad bosoms empty.
Macduff: Let us rather
Hold fast the mortal sword, and like good men
Bestride our downfall birthdom. Each new morn
New widows howl, new orphans cry, new sorrows
Strike heaven on the face, that it resounds
As if it felt with Scotland and yelled out
Like syllable of dolour.

                                        act 4, scene 3, lines 1–8

Malcolm, as we might expect, is cautious as he probes Macduff. It is a bitter irony that Macduff does not yet know he has lost his own family to Macbeth. "Downfall birthdom" is their native land, Scotland, which Macduff strongly vows to defend.

Malcolm: What I believe, I'll wail;
What know, believe; and what I can redress,
As I shall find the time to friend, I will.
What you have spoke, it may be so, perchance.
This tyrant, whose sole name blisters our tongues,
Was once thought honest: you have loved him well;

He hath not touched you yet. I am young, but something
You may discern of him through me, and wisdom
~~To offer up a weak, poor, innocent lamb~~
T'appease an angry god.
Macduff: I am not treacherous.
Malcolm: But Macbeth is.
A good and virtuous nature may recoil
In an imperial charge. But I shall crave your pardon;
That which you are, my thoughts cannot transpose.
Angels are bright still, though the brightest fell.
Though all things foul would wear the brows of grace,
Yet grace must still look so.

                                            act 4, scene 3, lines 8–24

Malcolm, shrewdly tentative, continues to sound out Macduff.

Macduff: I have lost my hopes.
Malcolm: Perchance even there where I did find my doubts.
Why in that rawness left you wife and child—
Those precious motives, those strong knots of love—
Without leave-taking? I pray you,
Let not my jealousies be your dishonours,
But mine own safeties. You may be rightly just,
Whatever I shall think.
Macduff: Bleed, bleed, poor country.
Great tyranny, lay thou thy basis sure,
For goodness dare not check thee. Wear thou thy wrongs;

The title is affeered. Fare thee well, lord.
I would not be the villain that thou think'st
For the whole space that's in the tyrant's grasp
And the rich East to boot.

act 4, scene 3, lines 24–37

Our sympathies divide between the Prince and the Thane, since their purposes are as one:

Malcolm: Be not offended;
I speak not as in absolute fear of you.
I think our country sinks beneath the yoke;
It weeps, it bleeds, and each new day a gash
Is added to her wounds. I think withal
There would be hands uplifted in my right;
And here from gracious England have I offer
Of goodly thousands. But for all this,
When I shall tread upon the tyrant's head,
Or wear it on my sword, yet my poor country
Shall have more vices than it had before,
More suffer, and more sundry ways than ever,
By him that shall succeed.

act 4, scene 3, lines 37–49

It may seem that Malcolm stretches his dissimulation too far, but as the son of the murdered Duncan he absolutely must be certain that Macduff can be trusted.

Macduff: What should he be?

Malcolm: It is myself I mean, in whom I know

All the particulars of vice so grafted

That, when they shall be opened, black Macbeth

Will seem as pure as snow, and the poor state

Esteem him as a lamb, being compared

With my confineless harms.

Macduff: Not in the legions

Of horrid hell can come a devil more damned

In evils to top Macbeth.

Malcolm: I grant him bloody,

Luxurious, avaricious, false, deceitful,

Sudden, malicious, smacking of every sin

That has a name. But there's no bottom, none,

In my voluptuousness. Your wives, your daughters,

Your matrons and your maids could not fill up

The cistern of my lust; and my desire

All continent impediments would o'erbear

That did oppose my will. Better Macbeth

Than such an one to reign.

                    act 4, scene 3, lines 49–66

This is so grandly preposterous that the heroic Macduff is curiously blind when he credits it. His response would be outrageous if it were not the norm for Scottish monarchs.

Macduff: Boundless intemperance

In nature is a tyranny. It hath been

Th'untimely emptying of the happy throne,
And fall of many kings. But fear not yet
To take upon you what is yours. You may
Convey your pleasures in a spacious plenty
And yet seem cold. The time you may so hoodwink.
We have willing dames enough; there cannot be
That vulture in you to devour so many
As will to greatness dedicate themselves,
Finding it so inclined.

It is almost comic that Macduff has to tell Malcolm that however vulture-like the Prince may be, a plenitude of damsels will be glad to gratify him.

Malcolm: With this there grows
In my most ill-composed affection such
A stanchless avarice that, were I king,
I should cut off the nobles for their lands,
Desire his jewels and this other's house,
And my more-having would be as a sauce
To make me hunger more, that I should forge
Quarrels unjust against the good and loyal,
Destroying them for wealth.
                    act 4, scene 3, lines 66–84

Malcolm is a very young man and his cunning is clumsy, but Macduff again fails to see what transpires. All he can venture is that Scotland has the foisons, or resources, to satisfy the Prince's supposed greed.

Macduff: This avarice
Sticks deeper, grows with more pernicious root
~~Than summer-seeming lust, and it hath been~~
The sword of our slain kings. Yet do not fear;
Scotland hath foisons to fill up your will
Of your mere own. All these are portable,
With other graces weighed.

"Foisons" are financial resources, and "portable" means just bearable.

Malcolm: But I have none. The king-becoming graces,
As justice, verity, temperance, stableness,
Bounty, perseverance, mercy, lowliness,
Devotion, patience, courage, fortitude,
I have no relish of them, but abound
In the division of each several crime,
Acting it many ways. Nay, had I power, I should
Pour the sweet milk of concord into hell,
Uproar the universal peace, confound
All unity on earth.

                                    act 4, scene 3, lines 84–100

In his tenacity, Malcolm ventures on hyperbolic absurdity, but then the stalwart Macduff is hardly able to tell the difference. One wonders why Shakespeare prolongs this severe testing. In defense, Macbeth's reign of terror justifies Malcolm's distrust of all the thanes. In any case, we have reached the climax:

Macduff: O Scotland, Scotland.

Malcolm: If such a one be fit to govern, speak.
I am as I have spoken.

Macduff: Fit to govern?
No, not to live. O nation miserable!
With an untitled tyrant bloody-sceptred,
When shalt thou see thy wholesome days again,
Since that the truest issue of thy throne
By his own interdiction stands accursed
And does blaspheme his breed? Thy royal father
Was a most sainted king; the queen that bore thee,
Oft'ner upon her knees than on her feet,
Died every day she lived. Fare thee well.
These evils thou repeat'st upon thyself
Hath banished me from Scotland. O my breast,
Thy hope ends here.

Malcolm: Macduff, this noble passion,
Child of integrity, hath from my soul
Wiped the black scruples, reconciled my thoughts
To thy good truth and honour. Devilish Macbeth
By many of these trains hath sought to win me
Into his power, and modest wisdom plucks me
From over-credulous haste. But God above
Deal between thee and me. For even now
I put myself to thy direction and
Unspeak mine own detraction. Here abjure
The taints and blames I laid upon myself,
For strangers to my nature. I am yet

Unknown to woman, never was forsworn,

Scarcely have coveted what was mine own,

At no time broke my faith, would not betray

The devil to his fellow, and delight

No less in truth than life. My first false speaking

Was this upon myself. What I am truly

Is thine and my poor country's to command.

Whither indeed, before thy here-approach,

Old Siward, with ten thousand warlike men

Already at a point, was setting forth.

Now we'll together, and the chance of goodness

Be like our warranted quarrel. Why are you silent?

Macduff: Such welcome and unwelcome things at once

'Tis hard to reconcile.

act 4, scene 3, lines 100–39

Aside from our relief that this episode is over, we can sympathize with Macduff's confusion. The entry of Ross brings the news of Macduff's grief:

Enter Ross.

Macduff: See who comes here.

Malcolm: My countryman, but yet I know him not.

Macduff: My ever gentle cousin, welcome hither.

Malcolm: I know him now. Good God, betimes remove

The means that makes us strangers.

Ross: Sir, amen.

Macduff: Stands Scotland where it did?

Ross: Alas, poor country,

Almost afraid to know itself. It cannot

Be called our mother, but our grave. Where nothing,

But who knows nothing, is once seen to smile;

Where sighs, and groans, and shrieks that rent the air,

Are made, not marked; where violent sorrow seems

A modern ecstasy. The deadman's knell

Is there scarce asked for who, and good men's lives

Expire before the flowers in their caps,

Dying or ere they sicken.

Macduff: O, relation too nice, and yet too true.

Malcolm: What's the newest grief?

Ross: That of an hour's age doth hiss the speaker;

Each minute teems a new one.

                                        act 4, scene 3, lines 159–77

To "hiss the speaker" is to express shock at the greatest atrocity
yet.

Macduff: How does my wife?

Ross: Why, well.

Macduff: And all my children?

Ross: Well too.

Macduff: The tyrant has not battered at their peace?

Ross: No, they were well at peace, when I did leave 'em.

Macduff: Be not a niggard of your speech. How goes't?

Ross: When I came hither to transport the tidings,

Which I have heavily borne, there ran a rumour

Of many worthy fellows that were out,

Which was to my belief witnessed the rather

For that I saw the tyrant's power afoot.

Now is the time of help: your eye in Scotland

Would create soldiers, make our women fight

To doff their dire distresses.

Malcolm: Be't their comfort

We are coming thither. Gracious England hath

Lent us good Siward, and ten thousand men;

An older and a better soldier, none

That Christendom gives out.

Ross: Would I could answer

This comfort with the like. But I have words

That would be howled out in the desert air,

Where hearing should not latch them.

Macduff: What concern they:

The general cause? Or is it a fee-grief

Due to some single breast?

The fee-grief is Shakespeare's coinage for a solitary desolation.

Ross: No mind that's honest

But in it shares some woe, though the main part

Pertains to you alone.

Macduff: If it be mine,

Keep it not from me, quickly let me have it.

Ross: Let not your ears despise my tongue for ever,

Which shall possess them with the heaviest sound

110

That ever yet they heard.
Macduff: H'm: I guess at it.
Ross: Your castle is surprised; your wife and babes
Savagely slaughtered. To relate the manner
Were on the quarry of these murdered deer
To add the death of you.

"Murdered deer" is a pun on deer and dear, making one wonder
about Ross's tone throughout the play. He made no effort to assist
Lady Macduff and her household, when he should have led them
in flight. There is a hint of something compromised about him.
He was somewhat tardy in deserting Macbeth, and is curiously
abstract in conveying the massacre to Macduff.

Malcolm: Merciful heaven.
What, man; ne'er pull your hat upon your brows:

This is a gesture of grief, in Shakespeare's time, but again it
manifests Malcolm's inadequacy.

Give sorrow words. The grief that does not speak
Whispers the o'er-fraught heart and bids it break.
Macduff: My children too?
Ross: Wife, children, servants, all that could be found.
Macduff: And I must be from thence? My wife killed too?
Ross: I have said.
Malcolm: Be comforted.
Let's make us medicines of our great revenge,

To cure this deadly grief.

Macduff: He has no children. All my pretty ones?

Did you say all? O hell-kite. All?

What, all my pretty chickens, and their dam

At one fell swoop?

act 4, scene 3, lines 177–222

The virginal Malcolm is of course childless, and cannot comprehend the full dreadfulness of Macduff's condition. There is a terrible pathos in "All my pretty ones?"

Malcolm: Dispute it like a man.

Macduff: I shall do so,

But I must also feel it as a man:

I cannot but remember such things were

That were most precious to me. Did heaven look on,

And would not take their part? Sinful Macduff,

They were all struck for thee. Naught that I am,

Not for their own demerits, but for mine,

Fell slaughter on their souls. Heaven rest them now.

Malcolm: Be this the whetstone of your sword. Let grief

Convert to anger; blunt not the heart, enrage it.

Macduff: O, I could play the woman with mine eyes,

And braggart with my tongue. But gentle heavens,

Cut short all intermission. Front to front

Bring thou this fiend of Scotland and myself;

Within my sword's length set him. If he scape,

Heaven forgive him too.

Malcolm: This tune goes manly.
Come, go we to the King: our power is ready,
Our lack is nothing but our leave. Macbeth
Is ripe for shaking, and the powers above
Put on their instruments. Receive what cheer you may,
The night is long that never finds the day.

act 4, scene 3, lines 223–43

There is a prolepsis of Macbeth's doom by the sword of Macduff. The act ends with an almost ludicrous juxtaposition of Malcolm's optimism and Macduff's tragic resolution. You can say that Malcolm attempts to be a free artist of himself but that he fails. Hegel first remarked that Shakespeare actually gives his great personalities spirit and imagination, and thus they can contemplate and see themselves objectively like a work of art, becoming free artists of their own selves. A. C. Bradley, in his splendid essay on Shakespeare and Hegel, illustrates this by citing the personality of Hamlet, who struggles against the difficulties of his own nature. Admirably, Bradley follows Hegel by negating conventional morality and emphasizing Macbeth's greatness of personality:

Is there not such good in Macbeth? It is not a question merely of moral goodness, but of good. It is not a question of the use made of good, but of its presence. And such bravery and skill in war as win the enthusiasm of everyone about him; such an imagination as few but poets possess; a conscience so vivid that his deed is to him beforehand a thing of terror, and, once done, condemns him to that torture of the mind on which he lies in restless ecstasy; a determination so tremendous and a courage so appalling that, for all this torment, he never dreams of turning back, but, even when he has found that life is a tale full of sound and fury, signifying nothing, will tell it out to the end though earth and heaven and hell are leagued against him; are not these things, in themselves, good, and gloriously good?

I always delight in this passage. It is in the high spirit of William Blake's Proverbs of Hell in *The Marriage of Heaven and Hell*:

> You never know what is enough until you know what is more
> than enough.
> Exuberance is Beauty.
> Sooner murder an infant in its cradle than nurse unacted desires.

Those three lines in particular resonate in juxtaposition with *Macbeth*. Breaking beyond all limits, Macbeth never knows what is enough until it is much more than enough. Despite his monstrosity, his exuberance renders him beautiful, in the aesthetic register. Blake meant that nursing unacted desires was infanticide, but Macbeth has a literal passion for murdering children.

Bradley takes aesthetic joy in Macbeth's courage in slaughter and in his tragic imagination, which so vividly prophesies what will be, and tells life's tale to its end in nothingness. I hear in Bradley's delight the accents of one of Macbeth's great descendants, Satan in *Paradise Lost*. I am moved to reflect that Hegel's slow, patient labor of the Negative is more than anticipated by Shakespeare. Macbeth's rapid, restlessly destructive labor of the Negative is a glorious good onstage, or when we read it.

The negative exuberance of a shuddering beauty returns with Lady Macbeth:

Enter a Doctor of Physic and a Waiting Gentlewoman.

Doctor: I have two nights watched with you, but can perceive no truth in your report. When was it she last walked?

Gentlewoman: Since his Majesty went into the field, I have seen her rise from her bed, throw her nightgown upon her, unlock her closet, take forth paper, fold it, write upon't, read it, afterwards seal it, and again return to bed, yet all this while in a most fast sleep.

Doctor: A great perturbation in nature, to receive at once the benefit of sleep and do the effects of watching. In this slumbery agitation, besides her walking and other actual performances, what, at any time, have you heard her say?

Gentlewoman: That, sir, which I will not report after her.

Doctor: You may to me, and 'tis most meet you should.

Gentlewoman: Neither to you nor anyone, having no witness to confirm my speech.

Enter Lady Macbeth, with a taper.

Lo you, here she comes. This is her very guise, and upon my life, fast asleep. Observe her, stand close.

Doctor: How came she by that light?

Gentlewoman: Why, it stood by her: she has light by her continually; 'tis her command.

Doctor: You see her eyes are open.

Gentlewoman: Ay, but their sense are shut.

Doctor: What is it she does now? Look how she rubs her
hands.

Gentlewoman: It is an accustomed action with her, to seem
thus washing her hands. I have known her continue in
this a quarter of an hour.

This somnambulistic vision of the once-fierce Lady Macbeth
is consonant with the Uncanny that pervades *Macbeth*. She has
become fixated on her part in the murder of Duncan:

Lady Macbeth: Yet here's a spot.

Doctor: Hark, she speaks. I will set down what comes from
her, to satisfy my remembrance the more strongly.

Lady Macbeth: Out, damned spot: out, I say. One; two. Why
then 'tis time to do't. Hell is murky. Fie, my lord, fie, a
soldier and afeared? What need we fear? Who knows
it when none can call our power to account? Yet who
would have thought the old man to have had so much
blood in him?

act 5, scene 1, lines 1–40

That last sentence never leaves my memory. It recapitulates:

Lady Macbeth: Had he not resembled
My father as he slept, I had done't.

act 2, scene 2, lines 13–14

One can wonder if Lady Macbeth is now haunted by patricide.

Doctor: Do you mark that?
Lady Macbeth: The Thane of Fife had a wife. Where is she
now? What, will these hands ne'er be clean? No more
o' that, my lord, no more o' that. You mar all with this
starting.

The butchery of Lady Macduff and her children fuses with the obsessive guilt of Duncan's murder. Endlessly washing her hands, lost in her trance, Lady Macbeth is living and dying several times at once.

Doctor: Go to, go to. You have known what you should not.
Gentlewoman: She has spoke what she should not, I am sure
of that. Heaven knows what she has known.
Lady Macbeth: Here's the smell of the blood still. All the
perfumes of Arabia will not sweeten this little hand. Oh,
oh, oh.

What remains will be suicide, hardly our expectation for this negative splendor of a woman.

Doctor: What a sigh is there. The heart is sorely charged.
Gentlewoman: I would not have such a heart in my bosom,
for the dignity of the whole body.
Doctor: Well, well, well.
Gentlewoman: Pray God it be, sir.

Doctor: This disease is beyond my practice: yet I have known
those which have walked in their sleep, who have died
holily in their beds.

Lady Macbeth: Wash your hands, put on your nightgown,
look not so pale. I tell you yet again, Banquo's buried; he
cannot come out on's grave.

act 5, scene 1, lines 41–64

Banquo joins the Macduffs and Duncan, and time's revenges
approach.

Doctor: Even so?

Lady Macbeth: To bed, to bed: there's knocking at the gate.
Come, come, come, come, give me your hand. What's
done, cannot be undone. To bed, to bed, to bed.

Exit Lady Macbeth.

That is the last time we hear her. The knocking at the gate
returns and there is an erotic poignance in the vision of Macbeth
and his Lady, hand in hand, going to their bed, which will be their
grave.

Doctor: Will she go now to bed?

Gentlewoman: Directly.

Doctor: Foul whisperings are abroad. Unnatural deeds
Do breed unnatural troubles. Infected minds
To their deaf pillows will discharge their secrets.
More needs she the divine than the physician.

God, God forgive us all! Look after her,
Remove from her the means of all annoyance,
And still keep eyes upon her. So, good night.
My mind she has mated, and amazed my sight.
I think, but dare not speak.
Gentlewoman: Good night, good doctor.

act 5, scene 1, lines 65–79

The hopeless outcry "God, God, forgive us all!" marks the exodus of Lady Macbeth from the stage of life.

CHAPTER 9

My Way of Life / Is Fallen into the Sere, the Yellow Leaf

After we see a number of the thanes and their soldiers marching toward Birnam, there to link up with Malcolm, Macduff, and an English army, Macbeth returns to the stage where we have not seen him for some time:

Enter Macbeth, Doctor and Attendants.
Macbeth: Bring me no more reports, let them fly all;
Till Birnam Wood remove to Dunsinane,
I cannot taint with fear. What's the boy Malcolm?
Was he not born of woman? The spirits that know
All mortal consequences have pronounced me thus:
'Fear not, Macbeth, no man that's born of woman
Shall e'er have power upon thee.' Then fly, false thanes,
And mingle with the English epicures.

act 5, scene 3, lines 1–8

With his customary defiance, Macbeth proudly cries out, "I cannot taint with fear." "Taint" may mean lose strength but there is also a sense of a coloring, as though fear would make him of ashen hue. "English epicures" is Scottish contempt for pleasure-seekers, in contrast to Caledonian ruggedness.

> Macbeth: The mind I sway by, and the heart I bear,
> Shall never sag with doubt, nor shake with fear.
> *Enter Servant.*
> The devil damn thee black, thou cream-faced loon.
> Where got'st thou that goose-look?

After an affirmation that he is resolute, Macbeth's reaction to the Servant shows a gathering frenzy:

> Servant: There is ten thousand.
> Macbeth: Geese, villain?
> Servant: Soldiers, sir.
> Macbeth: Go prick thy face, and over-red thy fear,
> Thou lily-livered boy. What soldiers, patch?
> Death of thy soul, those linen cheeks of thine
> Are counsellors to fear. What soldiers, whey-face?
> Servant: The English force, so please you.
> Macbeth: Take thy face hence.   [*Exit Servant.*]
>   Seyton, I am sick at heart,
> When I behold—Seyton, I say—This push
> Will cheer me ever, or disseat me now.

I have lived long enough: my way of life
Is fallen into the sere, the yellow leaf.

act 5, scene 3, lines 9–23

The astonishing power of Macbeth's language returns with his reaction to the push or advance of his enemies:

Macbeth: And that which should accompany old age,
As honour, love, obedience, troops of friends,
I must not look to have; but in their stead,
Curses, not loud but deep, mouth-honour, breath
Which the poor heart would fain deny, and dare not.
Seyton?

Enter Seyton.

Seyton: What's your gracious pleasure?

Macbeth: What news more?

Seyton: All is confirmed, my lord, which was reported.

Macbeth: I'll fight, till from my bones my flesh be hacked.
Give me my armour.

Seyton: 'Tis not needed yet.

Macbeth: I'll put it on.
Send out more horses, skirr the country round,
Hang those that talk of fear. Give me mine armour.
How does your patient, doctor?

Doctor: Not so sick, my lord,
As she is troubled with thick-coming fancies
That keep her from her rest.

Macbeth: Cure her of that.
Canst thou not minister to a mind diseased,
Pluck from the memory a rooted sorrow,
Raze out the written troubles of the brain,
And with some sweet oblivious antidote
Cleanse the stuffed bosom of that perilous stuff
Which weighs upon the heart?
Doctor: Therein the patient
Must minister to himself.
Macbeth: Throw physic to the dogs, I'll none of it.

                                        act 5, scene 3, lines 24–47

This is so brilliantly phrased that it takes an effort to remember that a murderous tyrant laments the madness of his beloved wife. Macbeth speaks for all of us, since who does not sorrow for the distress of an intimate partner? Our identification with Macbeth profoundly troubles me. Shakespeare uncannily subsumes all of us in relation to Macbeth. Every man feels a destiny however dimly perceived; every man feels wronged by life and needs to seize the moment; every man feels he needs to defend himself to the end against unjust and decided fate.

Come, put mine armour on; give me my staff;
Seyton, send out. Doctor, the thanes fly from me—
Come, sir, dispatch—If thou couldst, doctor, cast
The water of my land, find her disease,
And purge it to a sound and pristine health,
I would applaud thee to the very echo,

That should applaud again—Pull't off, I say.

What rhubarb, senna, or what purgative drug

Would scour these English hence? Hear'st thou of them?

Casting Scotland's water makes a dark metaphor for diagnosis by urine analysis. To scour is to purge, and suddenly Macbeth seems to need scouring himself. After commanding his armor to be put on him, he demands it be pulled off, an instance of mental confusion.

Doctor: Ay, my good lord; your royal preparation

Makes us hear something.

Macbeth: Bring it after me.

I will not be afraid of death and bane

Till Birnam forest come to Dunsinane.

act 5, scene 3, lines 48–60

The doubling of death and bane or destruction intensifies the mounting desperation of the usurping King of Scotland. Shakespeare abruptly moves to the invading joint forces of England and Scotland.

Drum and Colours. Enter Malcolm, Siward, Macduff, Siward's
Son, Menteith, Caithness, Angus and Soldiers marching.
Malcolm: Cousins, I hope the days are near at hand

That chambers will be safe.

"Cousins" may not mean kinsmen but simply friends. The "chambers" are bedrooms, now to return to safe harbors.

Menteith: We doubt it nothing.
Siward: What wood is this before us?
Menteith: The Wood of Birnam.
Malcolm: Let every soldier hew him down a bough
And bear't before him; thereby shall we shadow
The numbers of our host, and make discovery
Err in report of us.

This camouflage ironically undoes one prophecy of the Weird Sisters.

Soldiers: It shall be done.
Siward: We learn no other but the confident tyrant
Keeps still in Dunsinane, and will endure
Our setting down before't.
Malcolm: 'Tis his main hope.
For where there is advantage to be given,
Both more and less have given him the revolt,
And none serve with him but constrained things,
Whose hearts are absent too.

Those who could escape Dunsinane have done so; the remainder serve under duress.

Macduff: Let our just censures
Attend the true event, and put we on
Industrious soldiership.

The wary Macduff urges that just censures or judgments of Macbeth's waning force must wait for the conclusion of the coming battle.

> Siward: The time approaches,
> That will with due decision make us know
> What we shall say we have, and what we owe.
> Thoughts speculative their unsure hopes relate,
> But certain issue, strokes must arbitrate:
> Towards which advance the war.   [*Exeunt marching.*]
>
> act 5, scene 4, lines 1–21

The veteran Siward joins Macduff in modulating Malcolm's untried hopes. Authentic battle or strokes must arbitrate or resolve the outcome. Shakespeare magnificently turns to Macbeth and his last stand:

> *Enter Macbeth, Seyton and Soldiers, with Drum and Colours.*
> Macbeth: Hang out our banners on the outward walls;
> The cry is still, 'They come.' Our castle's strength
> Will laugh a siege to scorn. Here let them lie,
> Till famine and the ague eat them up.
> Were they not forced with those that should be ours,
> We might have met them dareful, beard to beard,
> And beat them backward home.
>
> act 5, scene 5, lines 1–7

Buoyantly Bellona's bridegroom, Macbeth's courage is at its height. "Forced" is to be reinforced by the thanes, who augment the English army, and compel the great usurper not to meet them man to man, "dareful" or strong in defiance.

> *A cry within of women.*
> **Macbeth:**   What is that noise?
> **Seyton:** It is the cry of women, my good lord.
> **Macbeth:** I have almost forgot the taste of fears.
> The time has been, my senses would have cooled
> To hear a night-shriek, and my fell of hair
> Would at a dismal treatise rouse and stir
> As life were in't. I have supped full with horrors;
> Direness familiar to my slaughterous thoughts
> Cannot once start me.
>
>   act 5, scene 5, lines 7–15

The unaccustomed fear ensues from intuiting the death of Lady Macbeth. Time, Macbeth's adversary, reminds him that his acute sensibility once would have gone cold with fear at hearing a shriek in the night. The hair on his skin, at hearing a dismal treatise or ominous tale, would have come alive. That is all past. Now direness or horrendous things cannot startle him.

> **Macbeth:**   Wherefore was that cry?
> **Seyton:** The Queen, my lord, is dead.

Macbeth: She should have died

    hereafter;

There would have been a time for such a word.

Tomorrow, and tomorrow, and tomorrow,

Creeps in this petty pace from day to day,

To the last syllable of recorded time;

And all our yesterdays have lighted fools

The way to dusty death. Out, out, brief candle,

Life's but a walking shadow, a poor player,

That struts and frets his hour upon the stage,

And then is heard no more. It is a tale

Told by an idiot, full of sound and fury

Signifying nothing.

                          act 5, scene 5, lines 15–27

I never recite these lines without remembering Ian McKellen's Macbeth. He rolled the fourteen "r"s in the twelve lines of this outcry so slowly that they seemed interminable. The burden of this sublime passage is ambivalent. "She should have died hereafter" hardly means that Lady Macbeth's death is untimely. At once Macbeth is saying that his wife would have died whether sooner or later, but also that she should have died at some moment in futurity, when her husband could have mourned her. Now there is no time for such a word or utterance. And then the great litany commences. Those endless tomorrows, which never will be, would have crept in so many feeble steps or passages until the final syllable or trace of remembered time. And all our yesterdays have shown fools or victims the way to dusty death. The brief candle of life is snuffed out. Life itself is but a bad actor, a walking illusion, who struts and frets or worries away his hour upon the stage, and then resonates no more. All of life becomes a story related by an idiot, whose tale, though full of sound and fury, signifies nothing. And with this terrifying eloquence, Macbeth embraces nihilism.

Shakespeare, at the zenith of his invention, proceeds to the outward manifestation of Macbeth's inward abyss:

Enter a Messenger.
Macbeth: Thou com'st to use thy tongue: thy story, quickly.
Messenger: Gracious my lord,
I should report that which I say I saw,
But know not how to do't.
Macbeth:　　　　　　　　Well, say, sir.
Messenger: As I did stand my watch upon the hill,
I looked toward Birnam, and anon methought
The wood began to move.
Macbeth:　　　　　　　　Liar and slave.
Messenger: Let me endure your wrath, if't be not so.
Within this three mile may you see it coming.
I say, a moving grove.
Macbeth:　　　　　　If thou speak'st false,
Upon the next tree shalt thou hang alive
Till famine cling thee. If thy speech be sooth,
I care not if thou dost for me as much.
I pull in resolution, and begin

To doubt th'equivocation of the fiend,
That lies like truth: 'Fear not, till Birnam Wood
Do come to Dunsinane,' and now a wood
Comes toward Dunsinane.

act 5, scene 5, lines 28–45

"I pull in resolution" might mean to retract or rein in, but "pull" probably should be emended to "pall" or fail. Powerfully, Shakespeare returns us to "equivocation" or dissimulation, here "of the fiend, / That lies like truth." "Lies like truth" could be an alternative title for *Macbeth*.

Arm, arm, and out.

If this which he avouches does appear,
There is nor flying hence, nor tarrying here.
I 'gin to be aweary of the sun,
And wish th'estate o'th' world were now undone.
Ring the alarum bell. Blow wind, come wrack,
At least we'll die with harness on our back.

act 5, scene 5, lines 45–51

We are taken beyond nihilism into cosmological devastation, when Macbeth, weary of the sun, desires the fabric of the entire universe to be undone. With desperate courage, he calls for the warning bell to be sounded. Let the wind blow, let wrack or ruin come. At least Macbeth will die in harness or armor, fighting to the end.

CHAPTER 10

The Time Is Free

The final scene gives us a solitary Macbeth, undaunted as ever:

Macbeth: They have tied me to a stake; I cannot fly,
But bear-like I must fight the course. What's he
That was not born of woman? Such a one
Am I to fear, or none.

act 5, scene 7, lines 1–4

He is a bear manacled to a post, and is hacked by dogs in a common public show, frequently held in theater arenas. Holding still to the equivocal prophecies, he can regard himself as immortal.

Enter Young Siward.
Young Siward: What is thy name?
Macbeth: Thou'lt be afraid to hear it.
Young Siward: No, though thou call'st thyself a hotter name
Than any is in hell.
Macbeth: My name's Macbeth.
Young Siward: The devil himself could not pronounce a title

More hateful to mine ear.

Macbeth: No, nor more fearful.

Young Siward: Thou liest, abhorred tyrant; with my sword

I'll prove the lie thou speak'st.   [*Fight, and Young Siward slain.*]

Macbeth: Thou wast born of woman.

But swords I smile at, weapons laugh to scorn,

Brandished by man that's of a woman born.   [*Exit.*]

act 5, scene 7, lines 5–14

The younger Siward is the final sacrifice to Macbeth's fury. Macduff, avenging counter-fury, seeks out the butcher of his family:

Macduff: That way the noise is. Tyrant, show thy face,

If thou be'st slain, and with no stroke of mine,

My wife and children's ghosts will haunt me still.

I cannot strike at wretched kerns, whose arms

Are hired to bear their staves. Either thou, Macbeth,

Or else my sword with an unbattered edge

I sheathe again undeeded. There thou shouldst be;

By this great clatter, one of greatest note

Seems bruited. Let me find him, Fortune,

And more I beg not.   [*Exit.*]

act 5, scene 7, lines 15–24

The wretched kerns are mercenaries, Macbeth's last defenders. Macduff, above all else, will not allow anyone but himself to immolate the usurper:

Alarum. Enter Macbeth.

Macbeth: Why should I play the Roman fool, and die
On mine own sword? Whiles I see lives, the gashes
Do better upon them.

Enter Macduff.

Macduff: Turn, hell-hound, turn.

Macbeth: Of all men else I have avoided thee.
But get thee back, my soul is too much charged
With blood of thine already.

Macduff: I have no words.
My voice is in my sword, thou bloodier villain
Than terms can give thee out.   [*Fight. Alarum.*]

Macbeth: Thou losest labour;
As easy mayst thou the intrenchant air
With thy keen sword impress, as make me bleed.
Let fall thy blade on vulnerable crests;
I bear a charmed life, which must not yield
To one of woman born.

                              act 5, scene 8, lines 1–14

The intrenchant air cannot be cut, akin to the delusion that
Macbeth himself is immune.

Macduff: Despair thy charm,
And let the angel whom thou still hast served
Tell thee, Macduff was from his mother's womb
Untimely ripped.

The caesarean section was common in the Renaissance. And so again Macbeth is victimized by the equivocation of the fiend, that lies like truth:

> **Macbeth:** Accursed be that tongue that tells me so,
> For it hath cowed my better part of man.
> And be these juggling fiends no more believed
> That palter with us in a double sense,
> That keep the word of promise to our ear,
> And break it to our hope. I'll not fight with thee.

As never before, Macbeth is frightened. We scarcely can believe that he could refuse to fight.

> **Macduff:** Then yield thee, coward,
> And live to be the show and gaze o'th' time.
> We'll have thee, as our rarer monsters are,
> Painted upon a pole, and underwrit,
> 'Here may you see the tyrant.'
>
> act 5, scene 8, lines 14–27

In utter contempt, Macduff suggests that Macbeth will be exhibited as a freak, and painted on a fabric hanging from a pole, humiliated at the front of a booth in a fair.

> **Macbeth:**   I will not yield,
> To kiss the ground before young Malcolm's feet,
> And to be baited with the rabble's curse.

Though Birnam Wood be come to Dunsinane,
And thou opposed, being of no woman born,
Yet I will try the last. Before my body
I throw my warlike shield. Lay on, Macduff,
And damned be him, that first cries, 'Hold, enough.'

> [*Exeunt fighting. Alarums.*]
> [*Enter fighting, and Macbeth slain.*]
> [*Exit Macduff with Macbeth's body.*]
>
> act 5, scene 8, lines 27–34

It is not clear whether we see Macbeth's death, as I distrust the stage direction of "Enter fighting, and Macbeth slain." That is a later tradition, which Shakespeare's text does not support. Macbeth dies offstage, so that at first we do not know how the duel concluded. To see the death would mar the splendid theatrical re-entrance of Macduff with Macbeth's head:

Macduff: Hail, King, for so thou art. Behold where stands
Th'usurper's cursed head: the time is free.
I see thee compassed with thy kingdom's pearl,
That speak my salutation in their minds;
Whose voices I desire aloud with mine.
Hail, King of Scotland.

> act 5, scene 9, lines 20–25

"The time is free" is our liberation and yet also our sorrow, for something in us may have died with Macbeth. There is a loss of imagination, pearl beyond price.

All: Hail, King of Scotland!   [*Flourish.*]

King Malcolm: We shall not spend a large expense of time

Before we reckon with your several loves

And make us even with you. My thanes and kinsmen,

Henceforth be earls, the first that ever Scotland

In such an honour named. What's more to do,

Which would be planted newly with the time,

As calling home our exiled friends abroad,

That fled the snares of watchful tyranny,

Producing forth the cruel ministers

Of this dead butcher and his fiend-like queen,

Who, as 'tis thought, by self and violent hands

Took off her life—this, and what needful else

That calls upon us, by the grace of grace,

We will perform in measure, time and place.

So thanks to all at once, and to each one,

Whom we invite to see us crowned at Scone.

[*Flourish. Exeunt omnes.*]

act 5, scene 9, lines 25–41

King Malcolm's final speech is hollow, in contrast to our shock that Macbeth is done. To the high imagination we shared with Macbeth, this is a diminishment. That the imagination should fuse so fully with tragedy is both our enrichment and our desolation.

And yet we *are* richer after we have reread *Macbeth* or seen it properly directed and played. I always recall James Joyce's response to the Desert Island question: "I should like to answer Dante, but I would have to take the Englishman because he is richer." Shake-

138

speare's bounty, like his Juliet's, is as boundless as the sea. The more you take, the more he has, for his invention and his love for his characters are alike infinite. Something in us dies with Macbeth: call it ambition or the iniquity of an imagination that does not know how to stop. And yet, for all his negativity, Macbeth's vitality survives in our hearts. We cannot love him, since we are not Shakespeare, but absorbing him heightens our sense of being.